for 11 - 14s

BOOK 3

CHRISTIAN FOCUS PUBLICATIONS

We believe that the Bible is God's word to mankind, and that it contains everything we need to know in order to be reconciled with God and live in a way that is pleasing to him. Therefore, we believe it is vital to teach young teens accurately from the Bible, being careful to teach each passage's true meaning in an appropriate way for the age group, rather than selecting a 'teen's message' from a Biblical passage.

© TnT Ministries
29 Buxton Gardens, Acton, London, W3 9LE
Tel: +44 (0)20 8992 0450 Fax: +44 (0)20 8896 1847
e-mail: sales@tntministries.org.uk

Published in 2002 by Christian Focus Publications Ltd.
Geanies House, Fearn, Tain, Ross-shire, IV20 1TW
Tel: +44 (0)1862 871 011 Fax: +44 (0)1862 871 699
e-mail: **info@christianfocus.com**
www.christianfocus.com

Cover design by Profile Design

This book and others in the series can be purchased from your local Christian bookshop. Alternatively you can write to TnT Ministries direct or place your order with the publisher.

ISBN 1-85792-706-0

TnT Ministries (which stands for Teaching and Training Ministries) was launched in February 1993 by Christians from a broad variety of denominational backgrounds who were concerned that teaching the Bible to children be taken seriously. The leaders were in charge of the Sunday School of 50 teachers at St Helen's Bishopsgate, an evangelical church in the City of London, for 13 years, during which time a range of Biblical teaching materials was developed. TnT Ministries also runs training days for Sunday School teachers.

CONTENTS

On the Way for 11-14s / Book 3

WEEK	SUBJECT	PAGE
	Joseph - overview	6
1	Relationships with his Family	8
2	Relationships with his Masters	12
3	Relationship with the King	14
4	Relationships Tested	17
5	Relationships Restored	19
6	Relationships Remembered	22
7	A Character Study	24
	People in Prayer - overview	26
8	Abraham	28
9	Solomon	31
10	David	33
11	Nehemiah	36
12	Jesus	39
13	Paul	42
14	Mary	43
	The Saviour of the World - overview	46
15	A Saviour Prophesied	48
16	'Saviour' - a word study	50
17	Why Did the Saviour Come?	52
	Is God Fair? - overview	53
18	Predestination	55
19	What About Those Who Have Never Heard?	58
	Learning From a Sermon - overview	60
20	How to Listen to a Sermon	62
21	Listening to a Sermon	64
22	Review of previous two weeks	65
	The Sermon on the Mount - overview	66
23	The Christian Character	68
24	The Christian and God's Law	71
25	The Christian and God	74
26	The Christian and Possessions	76
27	The Christian and Other People	79
28	The Christian Response	81

Contributors

Preparation of Bible material:
Wendy Barber
Thalia Blundell
Rachel Garforth-Bles
Annie Gemmill

Editing:
David Jackman

Activities & Puzzles:
Wendy Barber
Thalia Blundell
Rachel Garforth-Bles
Steve Johnson
Jennefer Lord
Nick Margesson

On The Way for 11-14s works on a 3 year syllabus consisting of 6 books. It builds on the 9-11s syllabus and introduces young teens to study the Bible in a way which is challenging and intellectually stretching. Because they are often unprepared to take things at face value and are encouraged to question everything, it is important to satisfy the mind while touching the heart. Therefore, some of the lessons are designed to introduce the idea of further Bible study skills, e.g. the use of a concordance, a character study, studying a single verse or a passage.

Lessons are grouped in series, each of which is introduced by a series overview stating the aims of the series, the lesson aim for each week, and an appropriate memory verse. Every lesson, in addition to an aim, has study notes to enable the teacher to understand the Bible passage, a suggestion to focus attention on the study to follow, a 'Question Section' and an activity for the group to do. The Question Section consists of 2-3 questions designed to help in discussing the application of the Bible passage. The course can be joined at any time during its 3 year cycle.

To prepare a Bible lesson properly takes at least one evening (2-3 hours). It is helpful to read the Bible passage several days before teaching it to allow time to mull over what it is saying.

When preparing a lesson the following steps should be taken -

1. PRAY!

In a busy world this is very easy to forget. We are unable to understand God's word without his help and we need to remind ourselves of that fact before we start.

2. READ THE BIBLE PASSAGE

This should be done *before* reading the lesson manual. Our resource is the Bible, not what someone says about it. The Bible study notes in the lesson manual are a commentary on the passage to help you understand it.

3. LOOK AT THE LESSON AIM

This should reflect the main teaching of the passage. Plan how that can be packaged appropriately for the age group you teach.

4. TEACHING THE BIBLE PASSAGE

This should take place in the context of simple Bible study. Do ensure that the children use the same version of the Bible. Prior to the lesson decide how the passage will be read, (e.g. one verse at a time), and who should do the reading. Is the passage short enough to read the whole of it or should some parts be paraphrased by the teacher? Work through the passage, deciding which points should be raised. Design simple questions to bring out the main teaching of the passage. The first questions should elicit the facts and should be designed so that they cannot be answered by a simple 'no' or 'yes'. If a group member reads out a Bible verse as the answer, praise him/her and then ask him/her to put it in his/her own words. Once the facts have been established go on to application questions, encouraging the group to think through how the teaching can be applied to their lives. The 'Question Section' is designed to help you when it comes to discussing the application of the Bible passage.

5. VISUAL AIDS

Pictures are very rarely required for this age group. A Bible Timeline is useful so that the young people can see where the Bible passage they are studying comes in the big picture of God's revelation to his people. You can find one at the back of this book. A map is helpful to demonstrate distances, etc. A flip chart or similar is handy to summarise the lesson.

6. ACTIVITIES AND PUZZLES

These are designed to reinforce the Bible teaching and very little prior preparation (if any) is required by the teacher.

BENEFITS OF ON THE WAY

- Encourages the leaders to study the Bible for themselves.

- Teaches young people Bible-study skills.

- Everything you need is in the one book, so there is no need to buy activity books.

- Undated materials allow you to use the lessons to fit your situation without wasting materials.

- Once you have the entire syllabus, there is no need to repurchase.

On The Way for 11-14s is designed to teach young teens how to read and understand a passage of Scripture and then apply it to their lives (see How to Prepare a Lesson). Before learning how to study the Bible they need to know what it is and how to find their way around it.

The Bible

Christians believe that the Bible is God's word and contains all we need to know in order to live in relationship with God and with each other. It is the way God has chosen to reveal himself to mankind; it not only records historical facts but also interprets those facts. It is not a scientific text book.

What does the Bible consist of?

The Bible is God's story. It is divided into 2 sections - the Old and New Testaments. 'Testament' means 'covenant' or 'promise'.

The Old Testament contains 39 books covering the period from creation to about 400 years before the birth of Jesus. It records God's mighty acts of creation, judgment and mercy as well as their interpretation through the words of the prophets.

The New Testament is made up of 27 books containing details of the life, death and resurrection of Jesus, the spread of the gospel in the early Church, Christian doctrine and the final judgment.

Who wrote the Bible?

The books of the Bible were written by many different people, some known and others not. Christians believe that all these authors were inspired by God (2 Peter 1:20-21, 2 Timothy 3:16). As a result we can trust what it says.

How can we find our way around it?

Each book in the Bible is divided into chapters, each one of which contains a number of verses. When the Books were written originally the chapter and verse divisions were absent. These have been added to enable the readers to find their way around. When written down they are recorded in the following way, Genesis 5:1-10. This tells us to look up the book of Genesis, chapter 5, verses 1 to 10.

At the front of the Bible is a contents page, listing the books in the order in which they come in the Bible. It is perfectly acceptable to look up the index to see which page to turn to.

Aids to teach the Bible passage

- Many of the lessons have activity pages that help to bring out the main teaching of the Bible passage.
- Packs of maps and charts can be purchased from Christian book shops.
- A Bible Time Line is useful to reinforce the chronology of the Bible (see back of this book).

Questions to aid in understanding

Periodically use the following questions to help the young people understand the passage:
- Who wrote it?
- To whom was it written?
- When was it written?
- What situation is being described? (if applicable)

To make a chart of the Bible Library enlarge the template below and photocopy as required. Draw 2 sets of shelves on a large piece of paper (see diagram). Label the shelves. Cut off the unwanted books from each set and write the names of the books on the spines. Glue the books onto the appropriate shelves in the order in which they appear in the Bible.

The Bible Library

Old Testament	New Testament
Law (5 books)	Gospels & Acts (5)
History (12 books)	Paul's Epistles (13)
Poetry & Wisdom (5)	Other Epistles (8)
Prophets (17 books)	Prophecy (1 book)

OVERVIEW
Joseph

Week 1	**Relationships with his Family** To discover what happens when relationships go wrong.	*Genesis 37:1-36*
Week 2	**Relationships with his Masters** To understand how to cope with unjust punishment.	*Genesis 39:1 - 40:23*
Week 3	**Relationship with the King** To see how God was working out his purposes through the circumstances of Joseph's life.	*Genesis 41:1-57*
Week 4	**Relationships Tested** To understand that admission of sin is required before forgiveness can be given.	*Genesis 42:1 - 43:34*
Week 5	**Relationships Restored** To understand that the offer of salvation must be accepted for reconciliation to occur.	*Genesis 44:1 - 46:7*
Week 6	**Relationships Remembered** To learn that God does not treat us as we deserve.	*Genesis 49:29 - 50:26*
Week 7	**A Character Study** To learn how to do a character study.	*Genesis 37 - 50*

SERIES AIMS

1. To learn that God is in control of events and uses them to fulfil his purpose.

2. To understand the need to respond to God's offer of salvation.

MEMORY WORK

You intended to harm me, but God intended it for good.

Genesis 50:20

Joseph

The story of Joseph is a picture of God's sovereignty and demonstrates the way in which God is able to use a seemingly impossible situation to further his own purposes.

Joseph was the eleventh son of Jacob and the first son of Rachel (Genesis 30:22-24). As a result he was Jacob's favourite (Genesis 37:3). This favouritism led to family disharmony, the brothers became so jealous that they hated Joseph and 'could not speak a kind word to him' (Genesis 37:4). Eventually the brothers seized their chance and sold Joseph into slavery in Egypt. Whilst in Egypt Joseph was unjustly imprisoned, but through all this we are told that God was with him (Genesis 39:2,21,23). After two years, through his God-given ability to interpret dreams (Genesis 40:8), Joseph was brought to the attention of the king of Egypt. Joseph's wisdom commended him to the king (Genesis 41:37-41) and he was made Governor of all Egypt. In this position he was able so to order the affairs of Egypt during the seven years of plenty that, when the seven years of famine came, Egypt, the surrounding countries and Joseph's own family were saved from starvation. The story ends with Joseph becoming reconciled to his brothers and his whole family settling in Goshen in the land of Egypt. Eventually Jacob died and was buried. Joseph's brothers then asked forgiveness for what they had done to him in his youth. Joseph reassured his brothers by pointing out that, although they meant it for evil, God meant it for good (Genesis 50:20).

Through the series we will discover how God changed Joseph from a spoilt, arrogant teenager into a man he could use, and how he used circumstances to get Joseph into a position where he was able to save.

PREPARATION

Genesis 37:1-36

LESSON AIMS

To discover what happens when relationships go wrong.

In returning to Canaan to be with his father, Isaac, Jacob had faced the anger of Laban (Genesis 31:26) and the fear of revenge by his brother Esau, but through all this he was aware of God's presence in his life (Genesis 31:5-7). God was protecting and blessing him, fulfilling the promise he had made to Abraham (Genesis 12:7; 35:9-12).

In the years following his return to Canaan Jacob moved around from Succoth to Shechem to Bethel, etc. Rachel died giving birth to the last of his 12 sons, Benjamin (Genesis 35:18), and Jacob and Esau were reunited at the deathbed of Isaac (Genesis 35:29). Family relationships within Jacob's household were strained. Joseph was becoming an increasing irritant to his brothers, doing nothing to play down the favouritism his father showed towards him. He probably saw it as his duty to report the slothful service of his 4 half-brothers to his father (Genesis 37:2), but his action only increased their resentment.

The brothers appear to be morally undisciplined, immature and cynical (see also Genesis 35:22), whereas Joseph is portrayed as being spiritually aware yet needing to learn humility and wisdom in the ways of the world.

Jacob had learned nothing from his own early experience of favouritism. Yet from these tensions of a family in crisis God was to forge a nation set apart for his own purposes, in fulfilment of his promise to Abraham.

37:2   Joseph was the eleventh son of Jacob but the first-born of Rachel, the wife Jacob had loved (Genesis 35:24).

Joseph's brothers, the sons of the 2 maidservants, were probably sensitive about their position, bearing in mind what had happened to Ishmael, the son of Sarah's maidservant Hagar (Genesis 21:9-21).

37:3   A tunic with long sleeves indicated the position of the wearer. He was not expected to do manual work - the long sleeves would have got in the way. It was a sign that Joseph, the first-born of the favoured wife, was Jacob's heir, even though he was younger than 10 of his brothers.

37:4   Favouritism led to jealousy and to hatred.

37:10   Jacob took offence, not knowing that Joseph's dominion over him would operate within the context of the family's sojourn in Egypt and would not involve any usurping of his patriarchal authority.

'Your mother' - Rachel was already dead (Genesis 35:19), so this probably referred to Leah.

37:11   Jacob's experience of God had taught him to allow for God's hand in affairs and for God's right choice among men. See also Mary's response in Luke 2:51.

37:12   Shechem was approximately a day's journey from Hebron.

37:15-17 Joseph was concerned about proper obedience. His brothers were not where they should have been, so he could have returned home and reported this to his father. Instead he looked for them.

37:18-20 Hatred led to attempted murder.

37:21   Reuben was the eldest son, and was therefore responsible for his brother's welfare.

37:25   Ishmaelites were the descendants of Ishmael. The term is interchangeable with Midianites in this context (v.28). The Midianites were also descended from Abraham (Genesis 25:1-6). They inhabited desert areas east of the River Jordan and were traders.

37:28   20 pieces of silver was the going rate for a slave.

37:29   Reuben was absent whilst this was going on.

37:31-32   The lie is implied even though it is not spoken.

37:34   Sackcloth was made from goat's hair and was an irritant. It was worn as a sign of mourning.

37:35   Jacob's reaction showed how disjointed family relationships had become; all his other children were no comfort compared with the loss of his beloved son, Joseph.

1. Bearing in mind Jacob's youth and his own experience of favouritism (see Genesis 25:27-28; 27:41) why is he a 'disappointment' in terms of what he should have learnt and obviously had not?

2. Trace the results of Jacob's favouritism shown in this passage, e.g. v.4,8,11,18ff. What were the effects of favouritism on the relationships between Joseph and his brothers and Jacob and his sons?

3. Joseph's brothers were 'economical with the truth' when they took Joseph's coat to their father. Why did they tell lies? What can we learn about our own behaviour from this?

A map of the area is helpful - see page 10.

Spoilt Relationships   Divide into pairs or small groups and ask them to make an alphabetical list of things that spoil relationships, one thing for each letter of the alpahabet. The things can be attitudes, behaviour or activities, e.g. anger, betrayal, criticism, discouragement.

Photocopy page 11 for each group member.

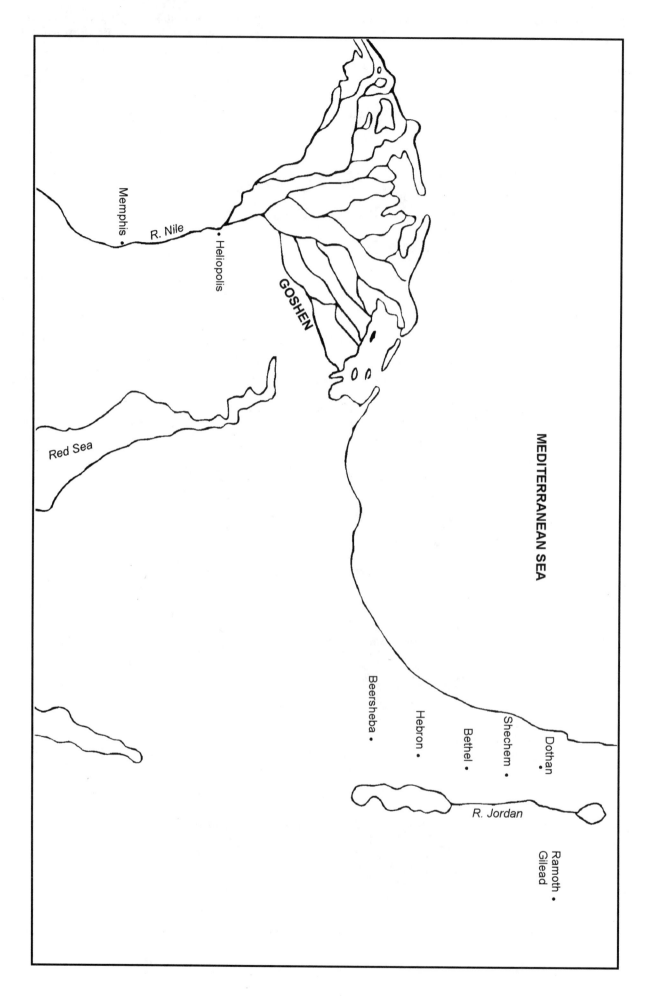

Memphis

R. Nile

Heliopolis

GOSHEN

Red Sea

MEDITERRANEAN SEA

Beersheba

Hebron

Bethel

Shechem

Dothan

R. Jordan

Ramoth
Gilead

Joseph's Family Tree

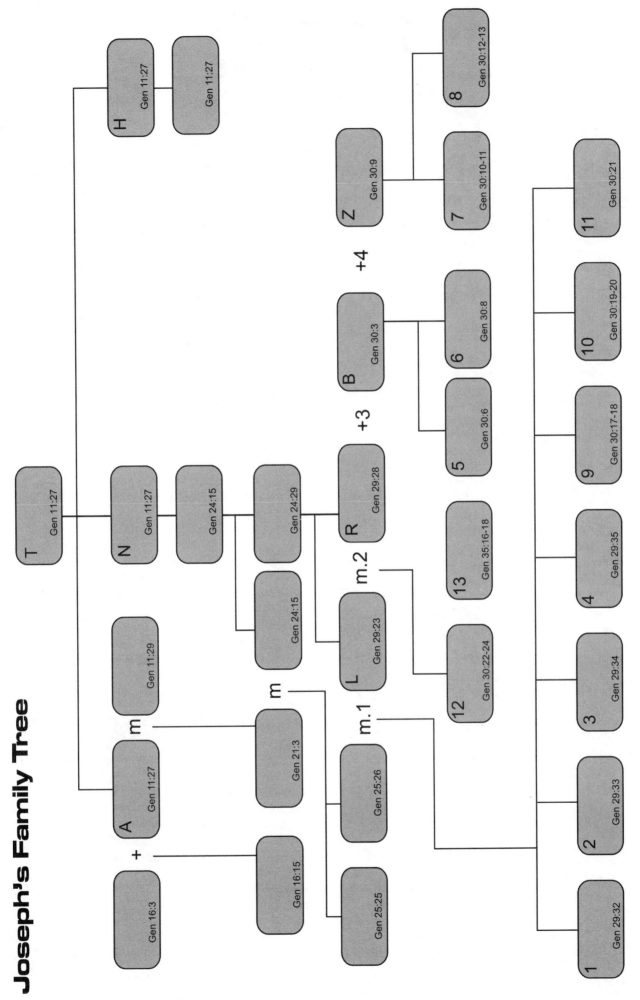

PREPARATION

Genesis 39:1 - 40:23

LESSON AIMS

To understand how to cope with unjust punishment.

39:2   Joseph had gone from being the favoured son and heir to being a slave, but God was still with him.

39:3-6   Joseph became a trusted slave of Potiphar and was appointed overseer of his house. The blessings that Potiphar's household received are an example of the overflow of God's covenant blessings. See also Jacob and Laban (Genesis 30:27).

39:6b-7,10   Joseph's temptation was constant and unremitting.

39:9   Joseph recognised that all sin is against God (see also Psalm 51:4).

39:10   Joseph not only said 'no' but also avoided the temptation whenever possible.

39:11-18   Joseph found himself in a no-win situation (v.14), because of the unsatisfied pique of Potiphar's wife.

39:20   Joseph was not executed, which was the usual punishment for his alleged crime. This may have been a reflection of the goodwill Joseph had earned by his previous service.

39:21-23   God was with Joseph in prison and Joseph was successful.

40:1   The cup bearer and the baker were high officials in Pharaoh's court.

40:3   The captain of the guard was responsible for the 2 prisoners. See 39:1 for the identity of the captain of the guard. Already God's hand can be seen controlling events.

40:8   Dreams were understood to be predictions of the future. Note how Joseph gave glory to God.

40:23   The cup bearer was restored to his original position and in all the rejoicing forgot Joseph's plea (40:14-15).

QUESTIONS

1. How did Joseph deal with temptation (39:8-10)? How does this help me when I am tempted to do wrong?

2. In the past 2 lessons on Joseph, has anything 'gone well' for him? Has he deserved any of the punishment meted out to him? How does he cope? What is your reaction to unjust punishment at home or at school?

3. These chapters repeat the phrase, 'the Lord was with Joseph'. What does that mean, and how does it apply to you?

FOCUS ACTIVITY

Unfair Forfeits   Either think of a selection of forfeits in advance or ask each member of the group to think of one each. Write each one on a piece of paper, fold up and place in a hat or other suitable container. Ask each group member a simple question in turn. The questions should cover a range of topics, some easily answerable and some not. Each answer is rewarded by a forfeit, even if correct.

At the end discuss how the people, who were given unjust forfeits, felt. Let's see how Joseph behaved when punished unjustly.

Charades (Give us a Clue)

Prior to the lesson choose suitable verses or words from the Bible passage for acting out.

Split the group into 2 teams. Allocate each team a number of words or verses. The teams take it in turns to act out the word or verse to the other side. Points are scored by the teams for correct answers.

Use the following actions to indicate what is being acted -

> Word - bring hand away from mouth once.
> Verse- bring the hand away from the mouth then, starting with the hands together in front of the mouth, part the hands to demonstrate length, i.e. more than one word.

This activity can also be done using drawings instead of actions.

PREPARATION

Genesis 41:1-57

LESSON AIMS

To see how God was working out his purposes through the circumstances of Joseph's life.

41:1   Note the time lapse.

41:14   The change of clothes and shaving were part of the Egyptian court custom.

41:16   Joseph gives God the glory - cf. Daniel 2:27-30.

41:29-31   The 7 years of famine are recorded in Egyptian historical records.

41:33-44   The court recognises the great wisdom of Joseph's answer. This, together with the interpretation of the dream, convinced them of Joseph's supernatural insight.

Joseph's office was probably that of Grand Vizier. Other non-Egyptians are recorded as having gained similar positions in Egypt in the period 2,000-1,000 BC.

41:38   Note the change in Joseph from chapter 37 - not only is he wise and discerning, but he is also 'one in whom is the Spirit of God'.

41:42   The gold chain and robes of fine linen signified Joseph's important position. The signet ring allowed him to sign papers in the name of Pharaoh.

41:45   Joseph made a cultural adjustment - he changed his name to an Egyptian one and married an Egyptian wife. However, he still kept his faith in the God of Abraham (v. 50-52). 'On' is Heliopolis.

41:46   Joseph was 17 years old when the story started. He is now 30. God had used those

years in slavery and prison to refine Joseph and prepare him for his position of power in Egypt.

41:53-57   It came to pass just as God said. God put Joseph in the right place at the right time and the Pharaoh listened and acted. The famine was severe and Joseph operated a system of famine relief, selling grain to the people of Egypt (v.56) and to other countries (v.57). Joseph's preparations had been well laid.

QUESTIONS

1. After a 13 year cycle of faithful service followed by wrongful punishment, Joseph suddenly became the Governor of all Egypt. How did he react to these gifts of great power, wealth and fame? How had his life since coming to Egypt helped to prepare him?

2. From the 3 lessons so far, sum up what has happened to Joseph and how he has changed as a result. Did these things happen by chance? How does this help me when circumstances appear to be against me?

3. The Egyptians realised that God was with Joseph (v.38). How do I know that God is with me? Look up John 14:23 to check your answer.

Life Events   Ask the group members to list key events and places in their lives, e.g. place of birth, places lived, schools attended, churches attended. Go round the group and compare the answers in each category. At the end point out that, despite all these differences, God has brought all of them to this place at this time in the day.

In today's Bible study we will see how God used the events of Joseph's life to prepare him for an important job.

Photocopy page 16 for every member of the group.

During Joseph's time in Egypt he was learning an important lesson. To discover what it was answer the questions below. The answers have been broken into groups of letters which can be found in the grid. As you answer each question cross off the relevant letters. When you have answered all the questions there will be 5 groups of letters remaining unused. When these are placed in the correct order in the spaces below the grid you will discover the lesson Joseph learnt. The first question has been done to start you off.

ALL	INC	SD	GOV	JOS	VEN
FAM	MAG	NI̶	DIS	PLE	ICI
SE	OM	ANS	WI	OW	GO
ROL	SW	RTY	EPH	INE	NOR
THI	NTY	ER	ED	ONT	L̶E̶

_ _ _   _ _   _ _   _ _ _ _ _ _ _ _

1. What was the name of the river by which the king was standing? (4) NILE
2. How many fat cows came up out of the river? (5)
3. What did the thin ears of corn do to the fat ones? (9)
4. For whom did the king send when he first woke up? (9)
5. Who was brought out of prison to interpret the dreams? (6)
6. The fat cows represented 7 years of what? (6)
7. The thin cows represented 7 years of what? (6)
8. What characteristic did the king say Joseph demonstrated? (6)
9. What position was Joseph given? (8)
10. How old was Joseph when he began to serve the king of Egypt? (6)

PREPARATION

Genesis 42:1 - 43:34

LESSON AIMS

To understand that admission of sin is required before forgiveness can be given.

42:4 Benjamin has taken Joseph's place as his father's favourite, the remaining son, so Jacob thinks, of his beloved Rachel.

42:7-17 Joseph tests his brothers to see if they have changed. He is not seeking revenge.

42:8 Joseph recognised his brothers - although at least 20 years had passed, they had been adults at the time they sold him to the Midianites.

They did not recognise him - he had been a teenager but was now an adult, in unexpected authority, wearing Egyptian clothes, shaven and speaking through an interpreter.

42:10 'My lord ..... your servants' cf. Genesis 37:8. The prophecy is fulfilled.

42:21 'How distressed he was .... his distress has come upon us' (cf. Galatians 6:7). They were realising their sin.

42:24 Joseph still loves his brothers (see also v.25-26).

42:36 Jacob dissolves into self-pity.

42:37 Reuben is prepared to take responsibility for his youngest brother.

43:3 'Judah said' - from here on in the story, Judah becomes the spokesman for his brothers. His tribe would become pre-eminent among the 12 and he would be an ancestor of Jesus (Matthew 1:2).

43:6 Note Jacob is called Israel - his covenant name. He is still blaming the 10 brothers for what has happened.

43:8-9 Note the change in Judah from 37:26-27.

43:11-14 God uses circumstances to bring Jacob to the point of capitulation - he must trust God for the future of his sons.

43:34 Joseph deliberately favours Benjamin - is this another test for the 10 brothers or is it a reflection of the way Joseph regards Benjamin (his full brother) as having special status? (See also v.29; 45:22.)

QUESTIONS

1. What changes are evidenced in the brothers, especially Reuben and Judah? How do they look back on the selling of Joseph (42:21-22)?

2. What response is needed from us before God can forgive us? Look up 1 John 1:8-9.

FOCUS ACTIVITY

Ladders Play the word game where one word is changed to another in steps, changing only one letter at a time. Each letter change must result in a real word. Show them how to change HAT to PIN: HAT, HIT, BIT, BIN, PIN.

Challenge them to change SIN into JOY. This could be done as individuals or in small groups. (SIN, BIN, BOY, JOY) If time permits, ask each group to design their own ladder and test it on another group.

Point out that there were steps to take to get from SIN to JOY. In today's Bible study we will see what steps need to be taken to get from sin to the joy of forgiveness.

This is a good story to act out. Split the group in half and ask each one to prepare a play from the Bible passage to act to each other. The play can be either the Bible story or a modern adaptation. Each group is responsible for organising themselves. They should appoint a director, who can then decide with his/her group on the script, apportion parts, etc.

PREPARATION

Genesis 44:1 - 46:7

LESSON AIMS

To understand that the offer of salvation must be accepted for reconciliation to occur.

44:1-5 The steward is in Joseph's confidence.

44:13 The brothers return to Joseph's house. This time there is no thought of deserting their father's favourite (see 44:10).

44:16 Judah recognises God's hand in the situation.

44:18-29 Judah relates the history of their dealings with Joseph.

44:30-33 Note the change in Judah. He is prepared to take personal charge of Benjamin, Jacob's favourite, and is keen to protect his father from further misery. He is willing to offer himself in place of Benjamin (see 43:9).

45:3 The brothers must have thought their last hour had come. (See 50:15-21 for what happened when Jacob died).

45:5 Joseph is conscious of God's hand in everything that had happened - but this did not mean that the brothers were not responsible for their actions (see 42:21-22).

45:10 Goshen is on the eastern part of the Nile Delta. It was a very fertile region then and still is to-day.

45:22 Benjamin is still being favoured.

45:24 Joseph gives his brothers a practical admonition.

46:1 Beersheba was the place where God appeared to Hagar (21:14-19) and where Abraham called on the name of God, the Eternal One (21:33). It was at the southern border of Canaan.

46:3-4 Note God's promise to Jacob.

QUESTIONS

1. Imagine how the brothers felt when Joseph revealed his true identity. Think about the explanations they would have to give Jacob. Truth must out - between all of them. What does God require from us when we come to him in repentance (Psalm 51:6)? Why?

2. Joseph reassured his brothers by telling them it was God who sent him to Egypt (45:4-8). Does this mean that the brothers were not responsible for their actions?

3. Before Jacob left Canaan God spoke to him in a vision (46:2-4). Why was this necessary? Look back to God's promises to Abraham (12:1-5) and to Jacob (28:10-15).

Happy Families   Play a game of Happy Families (e.g. Mr, Mrs, Master & Miss Drip the Plumber, Bun the Baker). The aim of the game is to collect complete sets of families. Deal out all the cards. The first person asks a particular member of the group for a specific card, e.g. Miss Bun the Baker's daughter. If that person has the card it must be handed over and the asker has another turn. If the person does not have the card it is his turn to play next. The person who collects most families wins. You need 1 pack of cards for every 5 or 6 people.

Ideally borrow proper sets of cards, otherwise use normal packs of playing cards, collecting sets of Jacks, tens, etc.

Let's see how Joseph's family were brought together again.

Photocopy page 21 for each member of the group.

The names are: Benjamin, Gad, Joseph, Issachar, Zebulun, Simeon, Levi, Judah, Abraham, Isaac, Naphtali, Dan, Asher, Rachel, Jacob.

The brother left out is Reuben.

By tracing a continuous path up, down and across through the word square, starting at the arrow, can you find Joseph and his relations? There are 15 names in all.

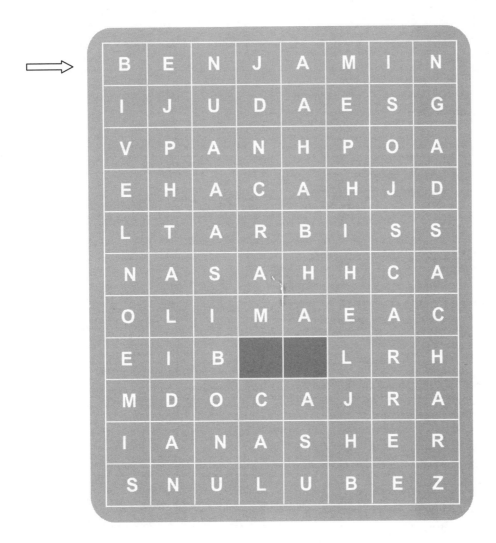

Which brother has been left out?   ....

PREPARATION

Genesis 49:29 - 50:26

49:29-32 Jacob has not forgotten that God had given him a homeland.

49:30 Mamre was at Hebron (23:19).

50:1 'Joseph wept' - he appeared to be an emotional and sensitive man. See Genesis 43:30; 45:2.

50:7-13 The journey is similar to that taken by the Israelites at the Exodus, 400 years later (see map on page 10).

50:15 'Holds a grudge ... and pays us back' - cf. Genesis 27:41, a similar story where Esau planned to kill Jacob as soon as their father Isaac died.

50:17 'Joseph wept' - maybe he was saddened by the thought that his brothers had not realised that he had truly forgiven them.

50:18 'Threw themselves down' - a fulfilment of Joseph's dreams (37:7), see also 42:6.

50:20 'God intended it for good' - Joseph sees and acknowledges God's overriding providence. All the nations around Egypt had come to buy food and God's purpose for Abraham's descendants was being worked out in their lives and times.

50:24-25 Cf. Hebrews 11:22. Joseph was looking forward to the 'Exodus'. Centuries later his bones were taken back to Shechem by Moses (see Exodus 13:19).

QUESTIONS

1. What does this passage teach us about forgiveness? Do we need to keep asking God to forgive sins already confessed? How should we

LESSON AIMS

To learn that God does not treat us as we deserve.

behave towards people whom we have forgiven?

2. Jacob called God his shepherd.(Genesis 48:15). Why was the shepherd picture such a comfort to him, and to us?

FOCUS ACTIVITY

Kim's Game Show a tray containing about 12 objects and give the young people 2 minutes to memorise everything on it. Remove the tray and ask each group member to write a list of the objects.

Point out that various things are remembered in today's Bible study. See if they can pick them all up as they go through the passage. The answers are: Jacob's burial wishes, the brothers' past sinful behaviour, Joseph's wishes regarding his bones.

VISUAL AID

A map of the area is useful - see page 10.

ACTIVITY

Photocopy page 23 for each member of the group.

The unscrambled sentence is: You intended to harm me, but God intended it for good to accomplish what is now being done, the saving of many lives. Genesis 50:20.

Unscramble the words in the sentence below to discover something Joseph had learnt and his brothers should have remembered.

OUY TNDDENIE OT ARMH EM TUB ODG DENNTIED TI FRO DOGO OT

SHPLICAOMC THAW SI WON GNIBE NODE TEH SNIVAG FO AYMN VILES

Which verse is it from?

PREPARATION

Genesis 37 - 50

LESSON AIMS

To learn how to do a character study.

This study should be used to sum up the life and character of Joseph, and to see parallels between him and Jesus. The brothers' actions and responses can be used to teach about how we should respond to the offer of salvation and forgiveness from God.

There is a lot of work to cover, so it may be wise to split the group into smaller units giving each group a section or two to research. The information can be pooled at the end in table form on a board/flip chart.

The information required
1. Family details, e.g. names of parents, brothers, sisters, etc.

    Genesis 29:20 - 30:24; 35:16-18; 41:45,50-52.

2. Place and type of dwelling.

    Genesis 35:27; 37:1; 39:2-4,20-23; 41:41.

3. Occupation and abilities/talents.

    Genesis 37:2,5,9; 39:2-6,20-23; 40:6-22; 41:25-44,46-49,53-57.

4. Other details, e.g. age, what he was like.

    Genesis 37:2-11,13; 39:6; 41:37-39,46; 42:18; 43:30; 45:9-11; 50:15-26.

5. Major events, e.g. sold into slavery.

    Genesis 37:19-28,36; 39:16-20; 41:37-44; 42:6ff; 43:15ff.

6. Strong points, e.g. obeyed his father.

    Genesis 37:13; 39:7-12; 40:6-8; 41:15-16, 37-39; 42:18; 45:4-8; 50:4-5.

7. Weak points, e.g. sneak.

    Genesis 37:2,6-10.

FOCUS ACTIVITY

Who Am I? Stick a label containing the name of a famous person on the back of each group member. They must guess who they are by asking questions of each other that can only be answered by 'yes' or 'no', e.g. Am I female?, Am I alive?

Discuss how much information was required for a successful guess. Let's see how much we have learnt about Joseph.

1. Summarise the change in Joseph from when he was a teenager in Canaan to when he was Governor of Egypt.

2. Draw up the following table to show the parallels between Joseph and Jesus and between the brothers and ourselves.

	Joseph	**Jesus**
Despised and hated	Genesis 37:4,8	Luke 4:24-30 Isaiah 53:3 John 1:10-11
Sold	Genesis 37:28	Matthew 26:14-16
Unjustly punished	Genesis 39:20	Luke 23:40-41
Raised to high honour	Genesis 41:39-40	Philippians 2:9-11
In a position to save	Genesis 45:7	1 Timothy 1:15
	The Brothers	**Us**
Recognised their guilt	Genesis 42:21-22	Romans 3:23
Unable to save themselves	Genesis 43:1-5; 44:16	Romans 5:8
Needed to accept the offer of salvation	Genesis 46:1-7	John 1:12

When doing the above activity we need to be very careful not to read in similarities that the New Testament does not warrant, e.g. Joseph's unjust punishment was only indirectly vicarious unlike Jesus'.

OVERVIEW
People in Prayer

Week 8	**Abraham**	*Genesis 18:16-33*
	To teach that we can pray to God, confident that he will do what is right.	
Week 9	**Solomon**	*1 Kings 8:14-61*
	To teach that God is worthy of praise and will hear his people when they pray to him.	
Week 10	**David**	*Psalm 51:1-19*
	To teach that God will forgive the repentant sinner.	
Week 11	**Nehemiah**	*Nehemiah 1:1-11*
	To teach that our knowledge of God affects the way we pray.	
Week 12	**Jesus**	*John 17:1-26*
	To see how Jesus prayed for himself, his disciples and future believers.	
Week 13	**Paul**	*Ephesians 1:15-23*
	To learn how to pray for others.	
Week 14	**Mary**	*Luke 1:26-56*
	To learn more about praise as a form of prayer.	

SERIES AIMS

1. To encourage the young people to know God better and to want to pray.

2. To help them understand more of what prayer is all about.

MEMORY WORK

Do not be anxious about anything, but in everything, by prayer and petition, with thanksgiving, present your requests to God.

Philippians 4:6

People in Prayer

These seven studies in prayer are designed to give insight into the practice of prayer as well as into the relationship between the praying person and his or her God. In the syllabus for both 3-9s and 9-11s the children will have studied the Lord's prayer and parables containing some of Jesus' teaching on the content of prayer and how to pray. In these lessons we are studying the different aspects of prayer. The following formula may be helpful -

A	Adoration -	Mary's prayer	week 14
C	Confession -	David's prayer	week 10
T	Thanksgiving -	Solomon's prayer	week 9
S	Supplication -	Jesus' prayer	week 12
		Paul's prayer	week 13

With Abraham (week 8) we reaffirm the teaching that God hears and answers the prayers of his people. Abraham was learning more about God through their dialogue about Sodom's destiny and Abraham's prayer was based on his knowledge of God thus far. His shock that God could act out of impulse (or so he thought), knowing God to be merciful and just, shows how well he knew his God. Nehemiah too knew God, knew his promises and trusted him to work according to his word. This expression 'knowing God' is crucial to understanding prayer and this is the main series aim.

It is not a question of just giving the group a formula which leaves them feeling guilty if they do not use it, but of encouraging them to pray and develop their relationship with God. As adults we know that prayer is work and Paul talked about 'wrestling in prayer' (Colossians 4:12b), but many of the youngsters come to God with a freshness and trust which must delight his heart.

PREPARATION

Genesis 18:16-33

LESSON AIMS

To teach that we can pray to God, confident that he will do what is right.

In this astonishing passage of Scripture we read of a divine soliloquy. God is portrayed as a man thinking and talking to himself. We know of course that his ways are not our ways and that his thoughts are beyond our comprehension, yet here is God wondering whether to involve Abraham in his plans for Sodom.

The passage follows on from the one where three guests (probably two angels and the Lord himself) have brought news of a son and heir for Abraham. The matter was not one for discussion, it had been dealt with, and in Genesis 18:10,14 the announcement is given, Sarah will have a son at the appointed time. The next matter is the future of the city of Sodom.

In these verses we see the covenant relationship Abraham has with his God, and the graciousness of God in allowing Abraham's voice to be heard.

18:16   Abraham knew the city of Sodom and some of its inhabitants, including his nephew, Lot. He had had dealings with the king of Sodom and rescued many citizens when war had overtaken them (see Genesis 14).

18:17   LORD - God's covenant name.

Abraham was called God's friend (see 2 Chronicles 20:7). He had been chosen by God to be the father of a godly household (18:19).

18:18   'Great and powerful nation' - cf. Genesis 12:2-3.

18:20   'Outcry' - a cry of righteous indignation against their sins. Chapter 19 is very explicit about the sins of Sodom, e.g. homosexuality (19:5).

18:21   'I will go down' - the result of God's intervention would be in judgment. This does

not mean that God does not already know everything, but is a way of saying that he does not act on a single complaint or out of ignorance.

18:22   'But Abraham remained standing' - this shows Abraham was able to talk to God directly.

18:25   Abraham's knowledge of the God's justness meant he could not understand how God could punish the innocent with the wicked.

18:27   'Lord' - note that Abraham does not use God's covenant name in his prayer. In contrast with God's exalted position Abraham knows his own unworthiness.

18:32   'Just once more' - it could appear that Abraham is haggling, but he is demonstrating a compassionate concern for his nephew and family.

QUESTIONS

1. Abraham's shocked response in v.23-25 was because of his prior knowledge of God. How does our knowledge of God affect the way we pray?

2. How does Abraham approach God in v.27?

3. Like Abraham, we are friends of God. What do we need to do to develop that friendship?

4. 'Thy will be done'. Was God's will done here in this passage?

Do the Right Thing   This is a version of the game 'Scruples'. Write on index cards a number of situations with a choice of actions. Read out the situation and ask the group members to indicate which choice they would make by raising a hand, standing up, moving to one side of the room, etc. It is best to do this as a group activity so that no individual is put on the spot.
Suggested situations:

1. You see someone drop a £5 note. Do you

   a) pick it up and give it back to them?
   b) hope that nobody else noticed and quietly pick it up when nobody is looking and keep it?

2. You pay for something in a shop and notice that you've been given too much change. Do you

   a) put it in your pocket and leave with a smile on your face?
   b) tell the shop asistant that they've made a mistake and return the extra money?

3. You accidentally break something at school which is discovered later on by a teacher. The teacher asks the person who broke it to own up. Do you

   a) ignore the teacher and hope that it is soon forgotten?
   b) own up and explain that it was an accident?

Discuss whether it is important to know that God will always do the right thing when we pray for things. Let's see what happened when Abraham asked God for something.

Photocopy page 30 for each member of the group.

There are no clues to the puzzle. First crack the code with the help of the given letters. When you have finished you will find that the shaded words make up a text from Genesis.

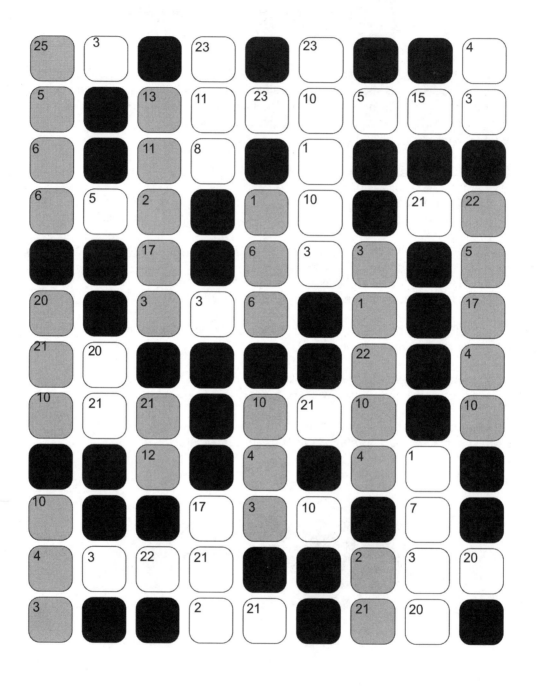

PREPARATION

1 Kings 8:14-61

LESSON AIMS

To teach that God is worthy of praise and will hear his people when they pray to him.

After 7 years of work the ark was brought from its temporary resting place and installed in the inner sanctuary of the temple built by Solomon. The whole building was filled with the glory of God's presence (8:10-11), in the same way as the cloud once rested on the tabernacle in the desert (Exodus 40:34-38).

These verses contain Solomon's reminder to the people of God's dealings with them and that God has fulfilled his promises, followed by his prayer of dedication.

Solomon's Declaration

8:15-16 God has kept his promise to David, to raise up his son to be the ruler of his people and to build the temple (2 Samuel 7:12-13). God is totally trustworthy.

8:17-19 God's instructions to David about the temple.

8:20-21 God has fulfilled his promise through Solomon. The temple is not just a place for the ark of the covenant but also a house for the Name of the LORD. In OT times God revealed himself to man through the names he used, e.g. Genesis 14:22; 16:13; 17:1; 21:33; Exodus 3:14-15; 17:15, Judges 6:24. Through his various names God revealed his character and sovereign purposes so that his people might have a relationship with him. God's name is, therefore, a shorthand way of describing who God is and what he has done.

Solomon's Prayer of Dedication

8:23-24 Praise and worship. Solomon focuses on God himself at the start of this prayer. 'No God like you' - no other god in history has performed the miracles and directed affairs to fulfil his covenant promise. The people of God are to continue **wholeheartedly** in God's way.

8:25-26 A prayer for God's blessing on the royal house. God's promise to David was dependent on David's descendants being careful to walk before God as David had done. So both ruler and people had to be committed to following God.

8:27-30 A prayer asking God to hear anyone who prays towards the temple. No building on earth could ever contain the God of heaven, but Solomon asks that God will hear the prayer and forgive the sin of his people when they pray towards the temple. This is to do with the temple being the place of God's Name and thus the place where God meets with his people to forgive them.

8:31-32 Asking God to judge between the innocent and the guilty. In the case of oath taking, an alleged offender was supposed to take an oath to prove innocence if there were insufficient witnesses. Therefore the blessings or curses which followed would establish innocence or guilt.

8:33-40 Asking God to forgive his people when they repent after God has punished them for their sins

- when defeated in battle (v.33-34)
- during drought (v.35-36)
- during famine, plague and siege (v.37-40).

Note that the end result should be God's people dwelling in God's land (v.34), living under God's rule (v.36) with a proper fear of God (v.40).

8:41-43 Asking God to hear and honour the prayers of the foreigner who turns to him, so that everyone in the world will know God's name and fear him.

8:44-45 Asking God for help in time of war.

8:46-51   Asking God to hear and forgive his people when they sin. Note the reference to exile (v.46) as well as the reminder of God's redemption of his people from Egypt (v.51).

8:52-53   Asking God to remember his servant and his people and grant their requests on the basis of his covenant promise (Exodus 19:3-6).

Solomon's Blessing
8:56   'Praise to the Lord who has given rest' - Solomon understood that this day was an historic event in the lives of the people after their travels and victories. Not one of God's promises has failed; God is faithful.

8:58   'Turn our hearts to him' - Solomon asks for God's help to enable the people to be faithful to the covenant.

8:60   The result of God's people following God wholeheartedly will be the recognition by all nations of the LORD being the only true God.

1. Break down Solomon's prayer into its different sections. What do they teach about Solomon's knowledge of God? Why is this knowledge a necessary basis for prayer?

2. Solomon asked God to hear when people prayed towards the temple. Does this mean that we should pray towards Jerusalem? If not, what does it mean?

3. What does Solomon's prayer teach us about the only basis on which we can come to God for forgiveness?

Hear, Hear!   Divide the group into 2 teams, A and B. The aim is for one team to direct a blindfolded member from one side of the room to the other without being tagged by the opposing team. The teams take it in turns and are timed. 10 second penalties are awarded for each touch by the opposing team. The team with the shortest time wins.

Team A blindfolds one member. Team B spreads out across the room. During the game each member of Team B can move only once taking up to 3 giant strides in any direction. The blindfolded player can only be tagged by a stationary team B player. Team A shout directions to their blindfolded player to get him or her to the finish line whilst avoiding team B players. Once the blindfolded person reaches the finish line the teams change over.

Discuss how difficult it was to hear the instructions, especially when several people were speaking at the same time. How important is it to know that God hears us when we pray to him? Let's see how confident Solomon was that God would hear his people when they prayed.

The following quiz should be done in 2 teams. The winner is the first team to get 6 gold pillars for the temple.

Requirements
Each team requires 8 pillars, 6 coloured gold and 2 of another colour. The pillars are randomly numbered from 1-8 on the back and are pinned to the board with the numbers showing. The other coloured pillars introduce an element of chance so that a team member who answers a question incorrectly will not place the team in an irretrievable position.

Rules
A question is put to each team in turn and, if answered correctly, one of the team members chooses a pillar by calling out its number. The pillar is turned over and, if gold, is pinned onto the board. A pillar of another colour is discarded.

If an incorrect answer is given the question is offered to the other team.

Allow 10-15 minutes for the quiz.

You need to work out a total of 16 questions from the Bible passage, 8 for each team.

PREPARATION

Psalm 51:1-19

LESSON AIMS

To teach that God will forgive the repentant sinner.

For the background to the lesson the incidents recorded in 2 Samuel 11:1 - 12:25 will need to be reviewed. Here was David, the greatest king of Israel, and a man after God's own heart (1 Samuel 13:14), falling into the sins of adultery, murder and duplicity with Joab. When Nathan the prophet confronted him, David made no attempt to play down his guilt (2 Samuel 12:13). The psalm is written in true repentance, asking for God's forgiveness, which was graciously given. Legally, David should have received the death sentence for adultery (Leviticus 20:10) and for murder (Leviticus 24:17). This he was spared, but he had to suffer the lifelong consequence of his sin in his relationships with his family and with Joab. However, he knew God's forgiveness, and he knew that it was to God he must go to obtain it.

51:1-2   'Mercy .... unfailing love .... great compassion .... blot out .... wash .... cleanse' - all of these David needs from God. 'Blot out' - here is the image of God keeping a record of events on a papyrus scroll, but then blotting out the record. 'Wash' - as with a filthy garment.

51:3   'Before me' - on my mind.

51:4   'Against you, you only' - David acknowledges that his sin was primarily against God.

51:5   David knows his own sinfulness through and through.

51:6   God requires us to be honest with ourselves.

51:7   Hyssop was used in ritual cleansing (see Leviticus 14:48-53). It was an aromatic plant with a straight stalk and white flowers. The hairy surface of its leaves holds liquids which made it suitable as a sprinkling device.

51:8   Joy, gladness and rejoicing are the outcome of forgiven sin.

51:10   'Create' - only God can make something out of nothing.

51:11   David remembers God's rejection of Saul (1 Samuel 16:1,14) and asks for God not to take away his Spirit, which was given to equip him for his royal post (1 Samuel 16:13).

51:13-15   David vows to praise God for his forgiveness and purification.

51:16-17   God does not delight in sacrifice unless it is accompanied by true repentance (see Amos 5:21-24).

51:17   A broken spirit and a contrite heart are the signs of true repentance.

51:18-19   A prayer for Zion from its king.

QUESTIONS

1. David was honest with God, with himself and with Nathan when confronted by his sin. Why do we often find it hard to acknowledge our sins?

2. What does this psalm teach us about David's knowledge of God? How did this knowledge help David turn to God in repentance?

3. How do we know that God forgives us? (1 John 1:8-10).

4. What is the only basis on which we can be forgiven? (John 3:16)

About Turn   Ask for volunteers and instruct them to obey your commands exactly. Line up the volunteers and tell them that you are going to march them towards an obstacle. (The obstacle can be a wall, chair, tray of cups of water, etc.) March the volunteers towards the obstacle calling out, 'Left, right, left, right,' and at the last moment shout, 'About turn!' Then march them away from the obstacle. See how close you can get to the obstacle before getting the volunteers to turn round.

This activity introduces the idea that repentance is about turning round and going in another direction. In today's Bible study we will see what happened when God faced David with his sin.

Photocopy page 35 for each member of the group.

David asked God for a 'pure heart'.

Fill the words of your memory verse into the grid, starting with the longest words. When you have done this, take the letters from the white circles and rearrange them to see what David asked God to give him.

Do not be anxious about anything, but in everything, by prayer and petition, with thanksgiving, present your requests to God.

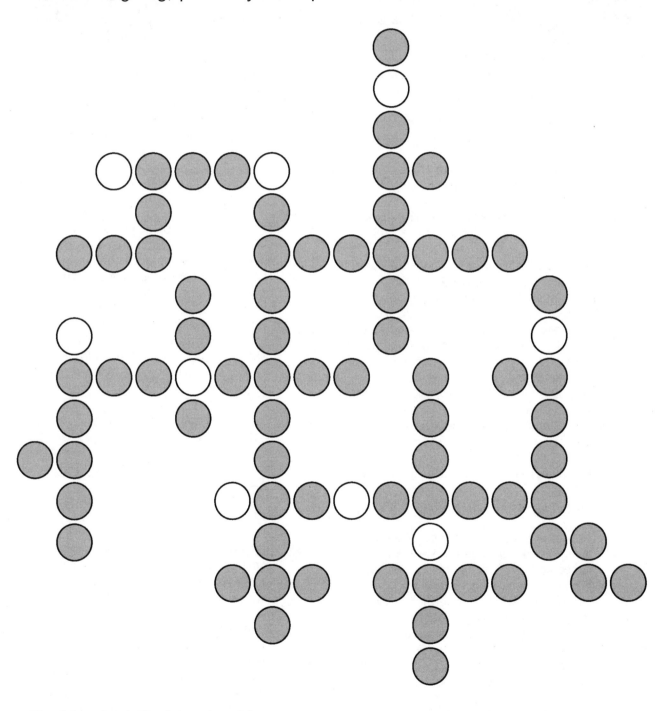

David asked God to give him a

PREPARATION

Nehemiah 1:1-11

LESSON AIMS

To teach that our knowledge of God affects the way we pray.

In the books of Ezra and Nehemiah three stages of the Jewish return to Jerusalem from exile in Babylon are outlined -

1. The main party returned with Zerubbabel in 539 BC to rebuild the temple, which was completed in 516 BC (Ezra 1:1-4).
2. A party of 600 returned with Ezra 78 years later to ensure that God's law was being taught and obeyed (Ezra 7:11-26).
3. Nehemiah returned in 445 BC to rebuild the walls of Jerusalem (Nehemiah 2:4-9).

In December 446 BC Hanani, who may have been Nehemiah's brother, brought sad news of the colony in Jerusalem. Nehemiah held a trusted position as a cupbearer to King Artaxerxes I in the Persian court. His job was to taste the king's wine in case it had been poisoned. The need for trustworthy court attendants was highlighted by the fact that Xerxes, the previous king, had been killed in his own bedchamber by a courtier. In the passage to be studied we read of how Nehemiah handles the bad news, and then works towards a solution for helping the Jews in Jerusalem.

1:1   Kislev was the ninth month of the Jewish calendar. Susa was the winter capital of the Persian kings in present day SW Iran.

1:2   Nehemiah questioned them about the Jewish remnant in Jerusalem. He was very concerned about his people and his land. When Jerusalem was destroyed, its people were either killed or taken into exile in Babylon and people from other nations were brought in to repopulate Israel and Judah.

1:3   Cities normally had high walls round them to protect the inhabitants, so the lack of city walls would mean that the people would be vulnerable to enemy attack.

See Ezra 4:7-23 for an account of why the walls were not rebuilt.

1:4   In OT times a god was understood to have power over a certain area and people, e.g. Dagon was the god of the Philistines. If country A defeated country B, A's god must be more powerful than B's god. The state of Jerusalem (the recognised place for the worship of Yahweh) therefore reflected on God's ability to protect his people, so far as the surrounding tribes were concerned.

Nehemiah's prayer

1:5   Praise and worship. 'Great and awesome God' demonstrates his reverential approach to God. By using the term 'covenant of love' Nehemiah is showing his confidence in God's love.

1:6-7   Confession. A true sense of God's greatness results in an awareness of the depths of our own sinfulness. Nehemiah confesses his own sin and that of his family and the people of Israel.

1:8-9   Trust in God's word. Nehemiah reminds God of his promise to bring his people back to their land if they turn back to him and obey his commands (Deuteronomy 30:1-5).

'Remember' is a key word in the book (See 4:14; 5:19; 13:31).

'Scatter' - the Jews were dispersed because of their unfaithfulness, just as God had said. By the NT period there were more Jews in the Diaspora than in Jerusalem.

1:11   Nehemiah prayed for the success of his plan. Four months later he had the opportunity to present that plan to the king in the form of a request to leave Susa and return to Jerusalem to see the situation for himself. This request was granted (see Chapter 2).

1. Look at the pattern of prayer used by Nehemiah. What can we learn from it? Look up Hebrews 10:19-22 and 12:28-29.

2. What was Nehemiah's motive for his prayer and on what did he base his prayer?

3. So far in this series we have seen that a person's knowledge of God affects the way he prays. Look back over the 4 weeks to see how that knowledge helped Abraham, Solomon, David and Nehemiah in their prayers. Where do we get our knowledge of God?

Did you know...? Give each person a pen and piece of paper and ask them to write down one true fact about themselves, which other people in the group might not know. Collect in the papers. Hand out a second piece of paper to each person. Read out the facts, one at a time, and ask the group to write down to whom they think that fact refers. At the end, read outh the facts again, in the same order, asking the person to whom each refers to stand up. The winner is the person who matches most facts to the right people.

Discuss the importance of knowing other people and how that knowledge might affect the way we relate to them. In today's Bible study we will see how Nehemiah's knowledge of God affected the way he prayed.

Photocopy page 38 for each member of the group.

Answer the questions and enter your answers in the grid. If you get the answers right the letters in the first column will spell the name of one of the people in the Bible passage. Try to do this without the use of your Bible. The verse numbers have been given if you get stuck.

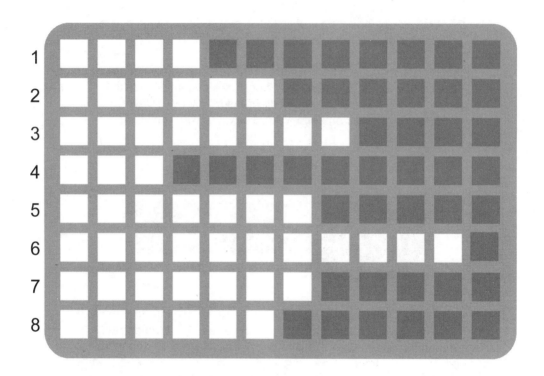

1. The temple in Jerusalem was a dwelling for God's what? (v.9)
2. A description of God's people. (v.9)
3. Nehemiah's father. (v.1)
4. Nehemiah asked God to let his what be attentive? (v.6)
5. What Nehemiah did when he heard the news about Jerusalem. (v.4)
6. What God gave Moses. (v.8)
7. A word used to describe God. (v.5)
8. Nehemiah's brother. (v.2)

PREPARATION
John 17:1-26

LESSON AIMS

To see how Jesus prayed for himself, his disciples and future believers.

Jesus had finished his life's work of passing on God's message. He had made God known and now there remained an awful death, but beyond it the glory he had laid aside to become a man. His followers would be left in a hostile, evil world. In this passage he prayed for himself, his disciples and for the future believers - the church.

Jesus' Prayer for Himself

17:1 'Father' - this term for God is used 122 times in John's Gospel.

'The time has come' refers to the time for his sacrificial death on the cross (cf. John 2:4).

'Glorify' - the glory of the Father and the Son are closely linked, and in his death Jesus would bring glory to God and bring people to eternal life.

17:2 'Eternal life to all those you have given him' speaks of God's initiative in salvation.

17:3 Knowledge of God is eternal life in the sense of being in relationship with God (cf. Jeremiah 31:33-34), so it is not just an academic knowledge but a personal relationship.

17:4 'I have brought you glory' - Christ's mission was not self centred. Jesus emphasised the supreme place of the Father.

Jesus' Prayer for His Disciples

17:7 'Everything .... comes from you' - the disciples had reached this stage in their understanding by seeing the Father at work in Jesus.

17:8 The disciples had responded in 3 ways:

a) they accepted Jesus' teaching (unlike the Pharisees)

b) they knew with certainty Jesus' divine origin

c) they believed (cf. John 1:12).

17:11 Jesus prays for unity and for protection for his disciples. True unity is only possible in God's name. God's name denotes his character, so true unity comes about through alignment with God's purpose to save the world through Christ.

17:12 The one doomed for destruction was Judas.

17:13-19 In John's gospel 'world' can mean the created universe, the people of the world, or those people or world systems that are hostile to God and God's people.

17:14 The world has a different mind set from God's people, who are children of light, sons of God, born of his Spirit.

17:15 Jesus does not pray that the disciples should escape from the world, but that the Father would protect them there. Their work is to be done in the world (v.18).

17:17 Sanctify means 'set apart for sacred use', or 'make holy'. Note the way in which they were to be sanctified (cf. John 8:31-32).

Jesus' Prayer for all Believers

17:20 Jesus is confident that the disciples will work and spread the gospel and, as a result, others will follow him.

17:21-23 Prayer for unity as in v.11. The result of true unity is that the world will believe as the disciples believed (v.8).

17:24 'Be with me where I am' - in heaven, which is the Christian's greatest blessing.

17:26 'Continue to make you known' - Jesus again speaks of relationship with God resulting from knowledge. Knowledge comes before experience, not the other way round.

QUESTIONS

1. From this prayer what do we see about the relationship Jesus had with his Father?

2. What does Jesus mean here about 'knowing God'?

3. Summarise what Jesus prays for himself, his disciples and his future church. Is there any link between all of these?

4. Does 'unity in the church' mean we all have to be and do the same? What does it really mean?

FOCUS ACTIVITY

Prayer Brainstorm Ask the group to shout out all of the different times when people might pray and the different things that people might pray for. You could introduce it by saying, 'If we went out into the street and asked people when they pray and what they pray for, what would they say?' Record the answers on a board, flip chart or large piece of paper.

Point out that most people pray at some time. Let's see how Jesus prayed and how it differed from the way we often pray.

ACTIVITY

Photocopy page 41 for each member of the group. The 5 letter word is 'cross'.

Solve the clues and write the answers in the grid. All the clues relate to the death of Jesus. If you get the answers right you should be able to find another 5 letter word in the grid.

1. Jesus' betrayer (John 18:2).

2. The number of the day of the week in John 20:1.

3. What Jesus brought to God (John 17:4).

4. Where Elijah drank (1 Kings 17:4).

5. It was made of thorns (John 19:2).

PREPARATION

Ephesians 1:15-23

LESSON AIMS

To learn how to pray for others.

QUESTIONS

Praying day by day for other people can be wearisome, but Paul found it a joy and seemed glad to pray for the Ephesian church, which, being one of his missionary congregations, he knew well. According to Acts 19:8-10 he was in Ephesus for over 2 years and the church there apparently flourished for some time. In this passage we see Paul's concern for the Christians at Ephesus, that they should realise God's power and purpose in their lives.

1:15   'Ever since I heard' - Paul is writing this letter from prison, probably in Rome, some years after the church was founded. It is thought that it was designed as a circular letter for other churches in the Ephesus area as well.

       'Faith .... and love for all the saints' were two characteristics that Paul was thankful to see. The love is faith in action (cf. James 2:14-17).

1:16   Paul had not stopped giving thanks for the Christians. He was continuously remembering them in his prayers.

1:17   Note the Trinitarian aspect of his praying. It is God's Spirit who reveals God to us so that we can know him better. Knowledge of God was of the utmost importance to Paul, as it was to Abraham, Solomon, David and Nehemiah (see previous lessons in this series).

1:18   Academic knowledge is not enough; our hearts must also be involved.

       The hope to which he has called us is heaven.

1:19-20   Paul prays for power for the believers, the power that will enable them to put their knowledge of God into action by living according to his will. This power is the same power which was demonstrated in the resurrection and exaltation of Jesus at the right hand of God.

1:22-23   cf. Philippians 2:9-11.

1. Compared to this prayer, our prayers for others are very mundane. Look at what Paul prays for the believers. How can we change our pattern of praying for others to make it more pleasing to God?

2. Knowing God is very important. How do we get to know God better, and how would this help us to pray for others?

FOCUS ACTIVITY

Friends   Ask the group members to write down on a piece of paper the answer to the following question:

'If you were offered 3 wishes (anything at all) that would be granted for a good friend of yours, what would they be?'

Make sure everyone completes the exercise. Ask people to read out their answers. Tell the group to hold onto their papers, because we are going to see how our priorities for our friends compare with Paul's.

At the end of the session get the group to compare their wish list for their friends with the prayer they will have written.

ACTIVITY

Try and write out a prayer for your Christian friends, which expresses what is best for them in their Christian life. This could be done in twos or threes.

WEEK 14
Mary

PREPARATION
Luke 1:26-56

LESSON AIMS
To learn more about praise as a form of prayer.

Praise and thanksgiving are closely linked to each other, and it is hard to draw a clear line of demarcation between them. Both consist of giving the glory to God. Thanksgiving is when we give God the glory for what he has done for us and praise is when we give God glory for what he is himself. With that definition praise lies on a higher plane than thanksgiving, but as we experience the grace and majesty of God as he has revealed himself to us, we realise that praise and thanksgiving overlap and complement each other.

1:26   Sixth month - refers to Elizabeth's pregnancy.

Angel Gabriel - one of the two angels in the Bible who are named. Gabriel also appears as the angel sent to Daniel (Daniel 8:16; 9:21), to announce the Christ who was to come.

Nazareth was called a city, as Greek has no word for town, only city or village.

1:27   'Pledged to be married' - the Jewish period of betrothal was a much more binding relationship than modern engagement and could only be ended by divorce. Bear in mind also that the concept of virgin birth is unique to Christianity. It has no parallel in other world religions. It could never have been invented by contemporary Judaism as it ran directly counter to all its preconceptions.

1:28-30   Mary is troubled not so much by seeing the angel but by what he has said, that she has been graciously chosen by God. Her reaction seems to indicate her unselfconscious humility and the deeply spiritual receptiveness of her heart.

1:31   Jesus is the Greek for Joshua, meaning Saviour.

1:32   Son of the Most High has two meanings -

a) the divine Son of God
b) the Messiah.

'His father David' - Joseph was in the Davidic line (see Matthew 1:6,16), as was possibly Mary also. So Jesus was both Son of God (Son of the Most High) and also a descendant of David.

1:34   How will this be? This was not a question of disbelief like Zechariah's (v.20) but a genuine response. She understood that Gabriel meant without human intervention.

1:35   Holy here means divine rather than morally pure.

1:38   Mary says she is God's servant (Greek = slave girl) and shows her complete obedience. This should not be underestimated. She would certainly carry a social stigma and suffer rejection by family and society, but she accepts God's will and is prepared to trust him.

1:39   The angel seems to have directed Mary to Elizabeth, so that Mary could share the joy, both natural and supernatural. There must have been tremendous relief in being able to open her heart to another woman, in all things like-minded, when such openness was not yet possible within her immediate family.

1:43-45   'My Lord' shows that Elizabeth recognises Mary's child to be the Messiah. This is a personal understanding. John, her child has to find out for himself. It is not until Jesus' baptism that he recognises Jesus as Messiah.

1:46-55   Mary's song or hymn of praise, sometimes called 'The Magnificat', which means glorifies. It is like a psalm and Mary's delight is not so much in the child she is about to have, but in God himself.

Mary's song is phrased largely in OT language. There are resemblance's to Hannah's song (1 Samuel 2:1-10) but without the bitterness. There is also a greater concentration on God's mercy in these verses. Mary knows she is a sinner and needs a Saviour.

1:46-47 Both soul and spirit are involved in the worship and glory of God.

1:49-51 Mary turns from thankfulness to think about God himself. She refers to three aspects of God's character. His power, his holiness and his mercy.

1:51-53 These verses detail the mighty deeds God has done -

> scattered the proud
> brought down rulers
> lifted the humble
> filled the hungry
> (spiritually and physically)
> sent the rich empty away.

1:54 God helped Israel by showing them mercy as he had promised.

1:56 'Three months' - evidently Mary stayed with Elizabeth until John was born and then returned to her home in Nazareth.

1. For what are you praised at school and at home? Is there a difference between thanking and praising someone?

2. Go through Mary's song of praise and list the attributes and deeds of God mentioned in it, differentiating between the two. What knowledge of God does Mary have? How does this knowledge affect the way she prays?

Paper Praise Bring in a pile of old newspapers and ask the group to go through them, cutting out all the headlines and articles where people are being praised. Stick them up on a board. (You might want to introduce an element of competition by dividing the group into 2 teams and seeing who can get the most/best headlines.)

When you have gathered a good number of headlines and articles, list on a separate large sheet of paper all of the things for which people have been praised. Tell the group that we will refer back to the list to compare it with the things for which God is praised in Mary's song in Luke 1.

At the end of the study make sure that the group understand how praiseworthy God is in comparison with human achievements.

Photocopy page 45 for each member of the group.

The 14 words in order are: glorifies, soul, spirit, God, saviour, humble, mercy, mighty, holy, hungry, scattered, lifted, filled, Lord.

By tracing a continuous path up, down and across, starting at the arrow see if you can find 14 words from Mary's song of praise in verses 46-56. Each word can only change direction twice.

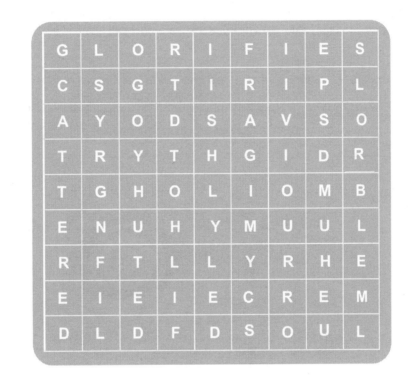

G	L	O	R	I	F	I	E	S
C	S	G	T	I	R	I	P	L
A	Y	O	D	S	A	V	S	O
T	R	Y	T	H	G	I	D	R
T	G	H	O	L	I	O	M	B
E	N	U	H	Y	M	U	U	L
R	F	T	L	L	Y	R	H	E
E	I	E	I	E	C	R	E	M
D	L	D	F	D	S	O	U	L

OVERVIEW
The Saviour of the World

Week 15 | **A Saviour Prophesied** *multiple OT references*
To see how the Old Testament prophecies were perfectly fulfilled by Jesus.

Week 16 | **Saviour - a word study**
To understand what sort of saviour Jesus is and to learn how to use a concordance.

Week 17 | **Why Did the Saviour Come?** *John 3:16-21*
To understand why we need a saviour and to learn how to study a Bible verse.

SERIES AIMS

1. To understand what sort of saviour the Lord Jesus Christ is and how he is the fulfilment of Old Testament prophecy.

2. To learn further Bible study skills.

MEMORY WORK

The Lord is patient with you, not wanting anyone to perish,
but everyone to come to repentance.

2 Peter 3:9

The Saviour of the World

The Old Testament contains prophecies about one who would come to save Israel. This salvation figure was called the Messiah (Anointed One), which is translated Christ in the New Testament. Salvation means deliverance from whatever is the trouble, e.g. enemies, disease, etc., and in the majority of Old Testament references the author of salvation is God, e.g. Hosea 1:7; 13:4,14.

In Exodus 6:6 God refers to himself as the redeemer of Israel (see also Isaiah 43:1-3). Under Levitical law the kinsman-redeemer was responsible for protecting the interests of the needy members of his extended family, for buying back (redeeming) land that a poor relative had needed to sell, for avenging the killing of a family member and for redeeming a relative sold into slavery (Leviticus 25:23-28,47-49). The great example of a kinsman-redeemer in the Bible is Boaz, whose role was studied in the series on Ruth (Book 1, weeks 24-28).

In Isaiah 49:1-7 the agent of salvation is the Messiah-Servant (see also Isaiah 53:4-6) and the salvation provided is of a moral and spiritual nature.

We need to remind the young people and ourselves that the God of the Old Testament is the same as the God of the New Testament. He has only ever had one plan of salvation for a needy world, but this plan is revealed in different ways at different times in history. The Old Testament contains the principles, e.g. suffering followed by glorification (Isaiah 53:10-12), but not specific details of the how, who or where (1 Peter 1:10-12). In the Sermon on the Mount Jesus told his disciples that he had come to fulfil the Law and the prophets (Matthew 5:17) and when he later appeared to his disciples after the resurrection he showed them that the Old Testament prophecies were all about himself (Luke 24:25-27,44-45).

In this short series we aim to discover how Jesus was the fulfilment of the Old Testament prophecies and what that means for us today. The second lesson of the series gives practice in the use of a Concordance and the third shows how to study a single verse. Both of these help increase our understanding of the sort of saviour Jesus is.

PREPARATION

See lesson notes for relevant Bible passages

LESSON AIMS

To see how the Old Testament prophecies were perfectly fulfilled by Jesus.

When looking at these prophetic passages with the young people it is wise not to get too bogged down in trying to interpret every detail. We need to remember that Biblical prophecy may have 3 levels of fulfilment:

   a.   at the time it was written,
   b.   at the time of Jesus,
   c.   in the future, when Jesus comes again.

Suggested lesson outline

A. Prophecies about the Salvation Figure

As you work through these passages the following questions need to be answered,

   1. What do we learn about the person of the saviour, e.g. where would he come from, would he be human?

   2. Whom would he come to save?

   3. What would he save from?

List your discoveries under the various headings.

Genesis

3:15   He would be human. Offspring is singular. Jesus is the offspring of the woman (Luke 3:23-38) and, although Satan would bruise his heel, ultimately Jesus would crush Satan's head (Romans 16:20).

          For the Saviour's humanity see also Isaiah 7:14.

49:10   Jacob is giving his sons his final blessings (49:1). These were recognised as prophetic.

          'Sceptre' - the symbol of kingship.

          'until he comes to whom it belongs' - the 'he' refers to the Messiah. (See also Psalm 72:8-11, which was recognised by the Jews as Messianic.)

The word 'Messiah' (Anointed One) was not a Patriarchal term, but this verse was given Messianic expectations later in Israel's history. It was understood to state that the Messiah would come from the tribe of Judah and would rule over all the nations.

Deuteronomy

18:15-19   He would be Jewish, ('from among their brothers'), and would be a prophet, (one who revealed God to the people). In these verses Moses is talking about when God gave his law to his people on Mount Sinai (Horeb). Moses acted as a mediator between God and God's people. The prophet who would come would be one like Moses (a mediator).

Isaiah

42:1   He will be anointed by God's Holy Spirit and will bring justice to the nations (the Gentiles).

53:10-12   He will be a guilt offering (see Leviticus 5:14-19). The salvation he provides will be moral and spiritual. He will deliver his people from sin and guilt, from judgment and eternal death.

          This salvation will be purchased by his death (v.12).

Jeremiah

23:5-6   'Branch' means shoot or fresh growth from the stump of a felled tree. This title is used for the Messiah in Isaiah 4:2-6; 11:1-9, Zechariah 3:8; 6:12-13.

          The Messiah's name, 'The Lord Our Righteousness', describes his character. In God's sight a righteous man is one who fully keeps God's law (see Job 1:8,22; 2:3,10). Thus, when the Messiah comes he will bring salvation to God's people (v.6).

These verses state that the Messiah would come from the line of David and would be righteous. He would also be a wise and just king and would save his people from their enemies.

33:14-18 These verses are a repeat of the ones above with the addition of the Messiah's priestly role. The Branch would not only sit on David's throne for ever, he would also continually offer the required sacrifices. (See also Zechariah 3:8; 6:12-13.)

Hosea
1:7 God will be his people's saviour. See also Isaiah 43:1-3.

13:4 God is the only saviour. Therefore the saviour must be divine.

13:14 Salvation is from the power of death.

Micah
5:2 Bethlehem Ephratha was a small town in Judah. See also Genesis 35:19, 1 Samuel 16:1.

'Whose origins are from of old, from ancient times' refers to the Messiah's family tree reaching back to the Patriarchs, as well as to him pre-existing his appearing. It infers his divinity.

5:3 Israel is to be abandoned to judgment until the Messiah is born. The Messiah will be born of a woman.

5:4 Messiah will care for his people as a shepherd cares for his flock (provision of water, food, protection, etc.). This shepherding is allied with kingship (see also Isaiah 40:10-11). Messiah's greatness will be world-wide.

5:5 Messiah will be his people's peace (Ephesians 2:14-16).

B. Was Jesus the fulfilment?
Go through the list and get the group to tell you how Jesus was the fulfilment of the prophecies.

C. What are the implications?
Make sure that enough time is left to discuss this section:

for the non-Christian - to accept Jesus as Saviour and King.

for the Christian - am I prepared to live my life under God's rule? What things need changing?

Recognition Give each person a pen and a piece of paper. Ask them to place the pens in their mouths and draw a familiar object on the piece of paper. They can use their hands to hold the paper still, but not to touch the pen. Once they have finished ask them to exchange their pieces of paper and try to guess what has been drawn. If they cannot guess they are allowed 3 questions that can only be answered by 'yes' or 'no'.

Discuss how easy or difficult it was to recognise the objects. What would have made it easier? Was the information gained from the questions helpful? In today's Bible study we will see what information God gave to his people so that they could recognise the Messiah when he came.

PREPARATION

See lesson notes for relevant Bible passages

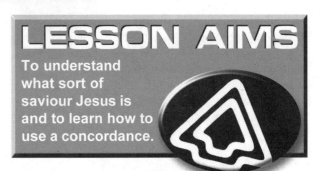

LESSON AIMS

To understand what sort of saviour Jesus is and to learn how to use a concordance.

NB a selection of concordances must be available for this lesson.

Suggested lesson outline:

Introduction

Try and get the group to define 'saviour'. A dictionary definition is - 'deliverer, redeemer, person who saves the state, etc. from destruction'. It is not a common word in everyday language, but we do use the verb 'to save' more frequently, e.g. saved my life, saved by the bell, saved up my money (kept for a purpose).

How to use a concordance

Explain what a concordance is - a list in alphabetical order of words found in the Bible. Under each heading is a list of Bible references in the order in which they appear in the Bible. Each reference is attached to a line from the verse so that the word can be seen in context. Explain the use of a concordance as a Bible study tool and that different Bible versions require you to use the appropriate concordance.

Demonstrate how to use the concordance by looking up 'saviour' as a group activity. When looking up the references in the concordance there are 5 questions which need to be answered:

1. What does a saviour do?
2. Who is the saviour?
   (includes other titles, e.g. Rock)
3. Who needs a saviour?
4. What do we need to be saved from?
5. What are we saved for?

When each reference has been found, ask the young people which of these questions is answered and how. The amount of time available will determine how much of the study is done as a big group and how much is done as small groups. Once the group is confident they know what to do you may want to split them into twos or threes and give each small group a few references to look up. Ask them to write down what

they learn from each reference about the saviour. After a set time bring the class back together again to report back on their findings. These should be summarised on a flip chart or board for easy reference.

Word study on 'Saviour'

The following are only some verses which have been selected from the long list in the concordance. Depending on the length of your lesson, this number could be either curtailed or lengthened with further verses of your own choice.

Deuteronomy

32:15   Jeshurun means the upright one, i.e. Israel. The title 'Rock' is often found alongside 'Saviour' in the Old Testament. The title 'Rock' signified that God was a sure defence for his people. God's people rejected their Saviour.

2 Samuel

22:2-3   This is from David's song of praise when God had delivered him from his enemies and from Saul.

Horn - see Exodus 30:10. Atonement was made on the horns of the altar by placing blood on it.

22:47-49   These verses tell us what who the saviour is and some things that he does. He is worthy of praise.

Psalms

25:4-7   David prays for God's covenant mercies when suffering affliction for sins and when enemies seize the opportunity to attack. The saviour is the one who shows the right way and guides in the way of truth.

68:19-20   The saviour bears our burdens and gives escape from death. These verses are looking at the moral and spiritual aspect of salvation - deliverance from sin and guilt, from judgment and eternal death.

79:9 Salvation includes forgiveness of sins. God saves us for his name's sake.

Isaiah
43:1-3 The Saviour is also the Creator. He purchased our salvation for us - we could not get it for ourselves.

43:11 There is only one saviour.

Luke
1:47 It is possible to have a personal relationship with the saviour - God, **my** Saviour.

2:10-11 The saviour has come for the whole world. The baby born at Bethlehem was the expected saviour.

John
4:42 The Saviour of the world - in the NT the expression occurs only here and in 1 John 4:14. It points to the fact that he is not only a teacher but also a Saviour and his salvation extends to the world.

Acts
5:31 The saviour is in heaven at God's right hand. He gives repentance as well as forgiveness of sins.

Philippians
3:20 The Saviour will come again.

1 Timothy
2:3-4 God wants all men to be saved.

2 Timothy
1:8-10 We are saved for holy living (v.9). The saviour has destroyed death.

We are saved by grace alone, not because of any merit of ours.

Titus
3:4-7 We cannot earn our salvation, it is an undeserved gift.

2 Peter
1:11 The saviour's kingdom is eternal.

The following 2 references do not contain the word 'saviour', but speak about 'saved'. you may want to add them at the end as they reinforce some points already made.

Acts
4:12 Jesus is the only way of salvation.

Ephesians
2:8-9 Salvation is a free gift, we cannot earn it. We are saved for good works.

What are the implications?
Do leave time for a discussion on the implications of what has been discovered.

1. How does the knowledge of what I have been saved from affect my attitude to God?

2. How should my life change, knowing that I have been saved for good works?

3. What difference does it make knowing that there is only one way of salvation (Acts 4:12)? How does this affect my attitude to non-Christian friends, Missions, etc?

Rescue Divide the group into teams. Each team must appoint a leader. Mark out an area at one end of the room to be an island, big enough for all the teams to stand on. Using rope or masking tape make a line across the room 5-6 metres from the island. The area between the line and the island is a moat. At one side of the moat is a causeway, which is the only way off the island. All the teams apart from the team leaders start on the island. An adult leader with a large box stands at the island entrance to the causeway to act as gaoler.

Each team leader is given a hula hoop attached to a 6 metre length of string. Scattered in the moat are scrunched up balls of newspaper (or similar), one for each team member on the island. Each team leader has to fish a ball out of the lake and throw it to one of his/her team members. One of that team can then be released from the island by handing the ball to the gaoler, who will allow that team member down the causeway to safety. All rescued team members help their team leader fish for balls. No one is allowed to place any part of their anatomy in the moat. Anyone who does so is returned to the island. The winner is the first team to rescue all its members.

When setting up this game make sure that the moat is not so big that the balls cannot be thrown across it.

Comment on how well the team leaders did as rescuers. Let's see what the Bible has to say about God's promised rescuer.

PREPARATION

John 3:16-18

LESSON AIMS

To understand why we need a saviour and to learn how to study a Bible verse.

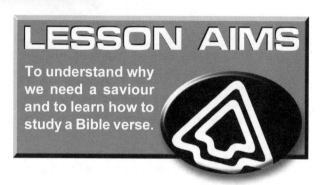

This lesson is one of an occasional series on how to study the Bible. Other lessons look at how to study a character (Jacob - Book 1, week 14 and Joseph - Book 3, week 7), how to study a word (Saviour) using a concordance, and how to study a passage (Acts 19:23-41 - Book 4, week 4).

When studying a Bible verse there are certain steps which should be followed. Use John 3:16 to demonstrate.

1. What is the context?

    Jesus is talking to Nicodemus, a member of the Sanhedrin, about being born again.

2. Who/what is the subject of the verse?

    God.

3. What does this verse say about the subject (descriptive words)?

4. What does the subject do (the verb)?

    (a) God loved

    (b) God gave.

5. To what/whom does the subject do it (the object)?

    What does God love?

    - the world.

    What is the world?

    - the created order (John 3:17a)?

    - all the people in the world (John 3:17b-18)?

    - what is opposed to God (Galatians 4:3, Ephesians 2:2)?

    Is there any more information about the object?

    - the latter part of the verse infers that the world is perishing.

6. What other information is present?

    E.g. Where, when, why, how, what result?

    What sort of love does God have for the world?

- he gave his one and only Son.

Who is the Son?

    - Jesus (Luke 3:21-22; 9:35).

Why did God give his Son?

    - to give eternal life to all who believe in him.

Do ensure that the there is proper understanding of the meaning of the words used in the verse.

Divide the group into twos or threes and give each small group one of the following verses to study:

    John 3:18, Acts 17:31, Ephesians 1:7, Ephesians 2:4-5, 2 Timothy 1:10.

After they have finished get the groups to feed back what they have done. Discuss why we need a saviour and what practical steps the group can take to bring their non-Christian friends to hear the gospel.

FOCUS ACTIVITY

Save us! Divide the group into teams. Each team chooses a team leader. Mark an area at one end of the room big enough for all the teams to engage in some sort of activity such as press ups or bicycling in the air. Each team leader starts at the other end of the room and has a set of 4 mats or pieces of newspaper. The team leader has to rescue his team using the mats as stepping stones. No more than 2 people can step on the same mat at any one time. Anyone who steps off the mat on the way to or from the island returns to the island. Whilst waiting to be rescued, the team members must continue with the designated activity. The first team to be rescued wins.

Discuss how well the rescues went. How glad were the team members to be rescued? In today's Bible study we will see from what we needed to be rescued.

OVERVIEW
Is God Fair?

Week 18 **Predestination** *Ephesians 1:3-14, Romans 8:28-38*
To understand the doctrine of predestination and how it affects my life as a Christian.

Week 19 **What About Those Who Have Never Heard?** *Romans 1:18-20; 2:1-16; 3:19-26*
To answer the question from a Biblical perspective

SERIES AIMS

1. To understand the doctrine of election and its implications for daily living.

2. To be reassured that we can trust God to deal with people fairly.

MEMORY WORK

God has set a day when he will judge the world with justice.

Acts 17:31

Is God Fair?

In this short series we will look at why we can trust God to treat people fairly. Young people are very concerned about whether or not things are fair and can be very vocal in their criticism of attitudes and actions they consider to be unfair. In the first lesson we will study the doctrine of predestination, which is difficult to come to terms with. Both human responsibility and divine election are clearly taught in Scripture, but they are truths that can never be fully grasped by the human mind. To try to 'balance' the two always leads to a Biblical imbalance. We have to hold both truths together. Almost certainly the group will react to this topic in such a way as to suggest that God is not being fair to choose some and leave out others. As well as dealing with the question of God's fairness, this lesson also provides an opportunity to discuss why we should evangelise and why we should live holy lives if God has already decided who will be saved.

The second lesson in the series looks at God's judgment on those who have never heard the gospel. It is hoped that, as well as reassuring the young people about God's fairness, this study will spur them on to tell their friends the good news about Jesus Christ. It is important to point out to the group that they **have** heard the gospel and will be judged accordingly. When talking about gospel issues we must not put undue pressure on individuals to respond; it is God who converts people, not us. However, it is our responsibility to present the gospel clearly and to ensure that the young people understand it, including the consequences of rejecting God's offer of salvation.

PREPARATION

Ephesians 1:3-14,
Romans 8:28-38

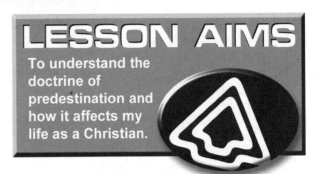

LESSON AIMS

To understand the doctrine of predestination and how it affects my life as a Christian.

As with all the apologetics style lessons the teacher's preparation is crucial. These notes are designed to give you some idea about how to approach the subject. How exactly you teach the lesson is up to you. The larger and younger the class, the more structured the lesson will need to be. The doctrine of election is a difficult one to come to terms with. Both human responsiblity and divine election are clearly taught in Scripture but they are truths that can never be fully grasped by the human mind. To try to 'balance' the two always leads to a Biblical imbalance. We have to hold both truths together. Almost certainly the group will react to this topic in such a way as to suggest that God is not being fair to choose some and leave out others.

The notes follow a suggested approach, but you may want to vary it with your group.

Introduction

1. Play a choosing game. Ask the group to divide into pairs and form 2 circles, with the partner in the inner circle standing in front of the partner in the outer circle. When the music starts the inner circle moves clockwise and the outer circle moves anti-clockwise. When the music stops those in the outer circle grab a partner from the inner circle. The partner must be different each time and different from the original partner. At each pause the leader gives an instruction for the pairs to follow, such as, 'Change left shoes,' or, 'outer circle give your partner your sweater,' etc. After 5 or 6 turns the group members find their original partners and are judged to see who is the oddest looking couple.

   Discuss how they made their choices. Today we are going to look at how God chooses people to belong to him. This doctrine is called Election or Predestination.

2. Define predestination - 'That work of God's grace whereby he chooses individuals and groups for a purpose or destiny in accordance with his will.' (*Bruce Milne* **Know the Truth** *IVP (1982) p.183*)

3. Where is the first mention in the Bible of God choosing someone?

   Abraham (Genesis 11:27 - 12:3)

4. How is this choice extended in Old and New Testaments?

   The nation of Israel, the chosen people (Deuteronomy 7:6-7; 9:5-6). Note that God's choice was not dependent on size or merit. Right from the beginning it was a manifestation of God's grace.

   The church (Acts 13:48, 1 Peter 1:1-2; 2:9-10)

What does the Bible teach?

This section could be done all together or by giving small groups different passages to research and feed back on.

1. **God is active in the world:**
   he sustains the world he made (Acts 17:24-28, Hebrews 1:1-3)

   he rules his world and directs all things to their appointed end (Psalm 115:3, Proverbs 16:9 - man, Amos 3:6 - natural events, Genesis 45:5 - evil).

2. **Proverbs 16:9**
   This verse contains the 2 elements

   - human choice (man plans)
   - predestination (God directs).

   The relationship between the two can never be fully grasped by the human intellect, but both are taught in Scripture so both are to be believed.

   The life of Joseph is one of the clearest descriptions of God's providence (Genesis 45:1-11).

3. **Ephesians 1:3-14**
   1:4   God chose people to belong to him before the foundation of the world. Salvation through Christ was always God's plan. It was not

changed by the Fall.

We are chosen to live holy lives. Holiness is the result, not the basis of God's choice. The Jews were not chosen because they deserved God's favour.

1:5   Chosen to be in relationship with him. Adoption was common among the Greeks and Romans, who granted their adopted sons the full privileges of their natural sons. Christians are adopted as sons by grace.

1:6   Chosen to bring glory and praise to God (see also v.12,14).

1:11   Chosen according to God's sovereign plan....

1:13   ... but we still have to respond to the gospel.

4.   Romans 8:28-38

8:28   God's people (those who love him) have been called (chosen).

8:29   Chosen to be conformed to Christ's likeness (live holy lives).

8:30   Eternal salvation. All who are called are eventually glorified.

8:33-38   Eternal security
- moral (v.33)
- physical (v.35-36)
- spiritual (v.37-38)

Tricky Questions

1. If God has chosen to save some, does this mean he has chosen to reject others (1 Peter 2:8)?

Whilst logically the election of some implies the rejection of others, Scripture is reluctant to set these 2 ideas in strict balance. Human responsibility is also taught - 'they disobey' (1 Peter 2:8). The doctrine of God's sovereignty has to be balanced with that of man's responsibility, which is to respond to the love of God shown in Jesus Christ.

See also 2 Peter 3:9 - God does not want anyone to perish, which is why the judgment is delayed.

2. If only some are called, does this make God unfair?

We can trust the God who knows everything to be totally fair (Genesis 18:25).

God does not need to save anyone, because all have sinned. God chooses to save some because he is gracious (Matthew 20:14-15 - the Parable of the Labourers in the Vineyard).

3. If God chooses the elect before the foundation of the world, aren't they bound to be saved regardless of what they do? Why bother to evangelise?

Romans 10:13-17, Matthew 28:19-20.

4. Is to foreknow the same as to foreordain? Can we say that predestination is just God knowing in advance how I will respond to the gospel?

This argument makes salvation a work, not a grace (Ephesians 2:8-9).

5. If I am one of the elect, does it matter what sort of life I live?

Deuteronomy 7:11, Romans 8:29, Ephesians 1:4, Colossians 3:12.

6. If God is at work in everything, does this mean that God causes evil and sin (Daniel 4:34-35)?

We need to distinguish between God's directive will and God's permissive will.

God's directive will refers to events that God sovereignly directs.

God's permissive will refers to events which God sovereignly permits.

This sounds great but is often difficult to apply in practice, as events which look disastrous at the time may not be so in the light of eternity, e.g. the cross.

7. How can a good and omnipotent God allow evil and sin?

Scripture recognises an ultimate mystery as far as evil and sin are concerned, i.e. we are not told how Satan fell into sin. However, the Bible does make clear that Satan's rebellion was to do with usurping the throne and function of God (not letting God be God) (Isaiah 14:12-15).

Evil = not good, i.e. contrary to God's declared mind and will.

The Bible is essentially a practical book. Evil is a fact of life, it has been overcome by Christ and it will be dealt with once and for all at the final judgment.

Man was made in the image of God and was, therefore, capable of resisting evil - but didn't (Genesis 3:14-19)!

Sin causes the suffering and tragedy we see in the world **but** my suffering is not necessarily a direct result of specific sins.

How do we reply to:

I prayed for healing from cancer, but God hasn't answered my prayers.

Why did God allow my mother to be killed in a car accident?

Points to raise are:
1. God's inscrutability.

2. We can have confidence in God's perfect character and will, as seen in Jesus.

Implications for daily living
1. God's providence implies that he has a controlling hand in our affairs, therefore we need to identify the many particular benefits and blessings which God gives us so that we can thank him for them.

2. The overall goal of God's providence is his glory and our good, i.e. the extension of his kingdom and our sanctification.

3. God's providence offers the Christian great security.

4. Recognition of God's providence does not absolve the Christian from the need to accept personal responsibility for his/her life. God is head over all things, but I am responsible to him for all I think and do.

Conclusion
1. The doctrine of election is a revealed truth, therefore we should accept it and believe it. God would not have revealed it if we did not need to know it.

2. It is a truth for the Christian and not an explicit part of the gospel to be preached to the unbeliever.

3. It must be held in tension with the Bible's teaching on human responsibility.

Suggested further reading :

John Stott **The Message of Ephesians**
Bible Speaks Today Series, IVP.

Bruce Milne **Know the Truth** IVP (1982).

PREPARATION

Romans 1:18-20;
2:1-16; 3:19-26

LESSON AIMS

To answer the question from a Biblical perspective.

As a background to the topic it would be helpful if the teacher would read Romans 1:18 - 3:26 through in one sitting, to get the thrust of Paul's diagnosis of sin and divine judgment.

The question, as with last week's, will probably raise the same response of 'it isn't fair!' Even for adults the doctrine is a difficult one to come to terms with, because real people spring to mind and the implications of the teaching are very serious. So it calls for gentleness in handling the topic. However, it can be used as a spring-board for understanding more of God's grace and unmerited favour to us sinners. It is suggested that Genesis 18:25 is a good verse to use to reinforce any discussion which follows.

1:18-20 No one has an excuse for not knowing God because he is evident in creation. Wrath is not an erratic outburst of anger, but God's just, holy abhorrence of all things sinful. God's judgment is being worked out in this world. See v.24,26,28 - he allows sin to run its own course here and now.

2:1-16 **The 3 principles by which God judges:**
1) v.2 based on truth. God is righteous and will judge rightly (Genesis 18:25).
2) v.6-11 our deeds. God holds each one of us responsible for our actions.
3) v.12-15 according to the knowledge or light a person has.

2:1 We have no excuse when judged by our own standards. We criticise others, and God will use those standards to judge us (cf. Matthew 7:1-2).

2:4 cf. 2 Peter 3:9. God is patient because he does not want anyone to perish. He delays the final judgment to give more time for repentance.

2:5 The day of God's wrath is the final judgment, as distinct from the judgment discussed in Romans 1:18-20.

2:6-7 We are not saved by our deeds, but by faith in what Christ has done for us. If we were judged by our deeds then no-one could be given eternal life. No-one is perfect, therefore none of us can earn our salvation.

2:12 The law is the Mosaic law. 'All who sin apart from the law' refers to the Gentiles. God will judge according to their 'light'. The group need to be pointed to the second half of the verse. They have heard God's law and will be judged by their response to his command to repent and believe the gospel.

2:14 By nature - or natural impulse. Pagans sometimes live morally upright lives, e.g. keeping faith with their marriage vows, helping the poor, etc.

2:15 Conscience functioned for pagans as the Mosaic law did for the Jews. It acted as a guide.

3:19 'Every mouth may be silenced and the whole world held accountable to God.' When God judges using the 3 principles studied above, no-one will be able to say it's not fair. Those who have not heard do not die because they have never heard but because of their sin.

3:21-26 In view of all that has gone before in the study the next verses come as a great revelation about the nature of salvation. Righteousness for Jews and Gentiles alike has come from God through faith in what Jesus has done. Here is the basis for salvation and here is the only way of being justified in God's sight.

NB a useful definition of justified is 'just as if I had never sinned'.

QUESTIONS

1. Can we trust God to judge **everyone** justly?

2. Is there anyone who has **no** knowledge of God?

3. How does God judge those who have heard the gospel?

4. What should our response be to those who have not heard the gospel?

FOCUS ACTIVITY

Its Not Fair! Play a game where people are rewarded for the wrong reasons. A suggested game is to stand the group in a line and see who can kick their shoe the furthest, highest, etc. Each time reward someone who has not achieved the task set.

Discuss how the group felt about the wrong people being rewarded. Is it important to be fair? Can we trust God to be fair? Let's see what the Bible has to say about the way God judges those people who have never heard the gospel.

OVERVIEW
Learning from a Sermon

Week 20	**How to Listen to a Sermon**	*Nehemiah 8:1-12*
	To understand why we need sermons and how to listen to them effectively.	
Week 21	**Listening to a Sermon**	
	To put the previous lesson into practice.	
Week 22	**Review of previous two weeks**	
	To hone the group's skills in listening to and learning from a sermon.	

SERIES AIMS

1. To learn what a sermon is and how to listen to one effectively.

MEMORY WORK

They read from the Book of the Law of God, making it clear and giving the meaning so that the people could understand what was being read.

Nehemiah 8:8

Learning from a Sermon

This series has been designed to teach young teens how to listen to a sermon in order to understand what is being said and learn from it. The previous series dealt with the acquisition of some Bible study skills, because we need to ensure that our teens are able to persevere in the Christian life when they leave us, by both feeding themselves from the Bible and being fed from the pulpit.

Many teenagers find the transition from youth group to the general fellowship a difficult one and this can be the time when we lose them. A comment often heard is that they learn more from their youth Bible study than they do by staying in church for the sermon. We need to teach them why God's word is taught in the form of a sermon and how this differs from the way it is taught in small group Bible study.

WEEK 20
How to Listen to a Sermon

PREPARATION

Nehemiah 8:1-12,
1 Corinthians 2:1-5

LESSON AIMS

To understand why we need sermons and how to listen to them effectively.

Nehemiah

8:1 The request comes from the people.

8:2 The word of God was for everyone, not just for a special few.

8:8 God's word was explained to the people so that they could understand it.

8:9 The people responded to what they had heard. Cf. 2 Kings 22:10-11.

8:12 Note the importance of understanding God's word (see also v.8-9). This understanding should be evident in our lives.

1 Corinthians

2:1 'Eloquence' refers to the manner of preaching.

'Superior wisdom' refers to the content of the message (see also 1:17).

2:4 Paul had renounced the manipulative methods of persuasion used in Greek rhetoric.

Suggested lesson outline

1. What is a sermon?

♦ Start with the focus activity.

♦ Ask the group to define 'sermon'. A dictionary definition is: 'a discourse usually based on Scripture and delivered from a pulpit by way of religious instruction or exhortation; similar discourse on religious or moral subject delivered elsewhere or published'.

♦ Study the 2 Bible passages above, then discuss the definition and amend as appropriate.

♦ Discuss what a sermon is/is not:

- not an entertainment or a sideshow (1 Corinthians 2:1-2). There must be a Bible content. The preacher's eloquence and a lively worship content can attract people, but cannot keep a congregation forever. We live in a culture where packaging is perceived to be more important than content, so must ensure that our young people recognise that content is more important than packaging.

- not a lecture (1 Corinthians 2:4-5). The preacher does not just impart information, but proclaims the life-changing word of God. The mind must be fed, the heart engaged and the will activated by the Word of God.

- a good sermon includes information giving and attracts the attention of the listeners, but its primary purpose is to persuade people to obey God's word, resulting in changed lives (Nehemiah 8:8-12).

2. Why do we need sermons?

It is important for the young people to understand how a sermon differs from a Bible study and why the Bible should be taught in this way.

♦ God's word needs to be heard to bring about change. For the written word to fulfil its purpose, the people to whom it is addressed must hear it (Romans 10:12-15).

♦ Reading Scripture aloud was an important part of congregational gatherings in both Old and New Testaments (Nehemiah 8:1-12, Luke 4:16-17, 1 Timothy 4:13).

♦ Jesus' priority was preaching (Mark 1:38; 3:14; 16:15).

♦ In the New Testament preaching is the core method for gospel proclamation (1 Corinthians 1:17-25; 2:1-5).

- Sermons should be preached, not read. Reading out a sermon is less effective than preaching it, because spoken language is different from written in its sentence construction and the words used.

- Sermons differ from group Bible studies in that a Bible study is a time of sharing what has been learnt, whereas a sermon declares God's word and calls for a response.

- Personal Bible study differs from a sermon in that, when I read the Bible, I am in charge of what I read, whereas when I listen to a sermon the person preaching is in charge and I am under his authority.

3. How can we listen to a sermon?

- There is no one right way to preach a sermon - no two speakers will give a talk in the same way. Preachers are not robots - their personality should come over in the sermon.

- A typical sermon has a:

beginning - includes the passage of Scripture being studied, (this may have been read beforehand), and an introduction to the topic.

middle - a number of points (often 3!) bringing out the meaning of the passage,

- illustrations to aid understanding and make the points memorable.

end - a summary of what has been said,

- personal application and/or challenge (this may have occurred at the end of each point).

- Have the Bible open at the appropriate place and use it to follow / check out what the preacher is saying.

- Taking notes helps you remember what has been said and allows you to review it at a later date. It is helpful to have a notebook set aside for sermon notes.

- Note taking is an art - it is not possible to record every word. The following is a suggested format:

  - title and Bible passage (+/- date and preacher).

  - main theme (there is usually one overriding theme, broken down into easily digestible sections, regardless of the number of points).

  - any headings used (these act as signposts).

- how the main points fit together. Include specific Bible verses from the passage plus any cross references.

- any illustrations that clarify the point being made.

- any applications.

- It is helpful to use your notes alongside the Bible passage to review what has been said before too many days have passed.

Can you hear me? Divide the group into teams. Make a barrier across the middle of the room. One member of each team is blindfolded and gets down on hands and knees on one side of the barrier. The remaining members of each team stand on the other side of the barrier. Blown-up balloons are placed on the floor behind the blindfolded players. The teams shout instructions to their blindfolded players to enable them to collect the balloons. Every balloon collected is passed to a leader, who keeps the score and takes that balloon out of play. A point is given for each balloon collected. No points are awarded for burst balloons. The team that collects most balloons wins.

Point out the importance of listening to the shouted commands and responding appropriately if the team was to win. Today we are going to look at how we should listen to a sermon.

WEEK 21
Listening to a Sermon

PREPARATION

N/A

LESSON AIMS

To put the previous lesson into practice.

Leaders should meet their groups prior to the church service so that they can sit together. Ensure that everyone has a pen and notebook for note taking, as well as access to a Bible.

At the end of the service suggest that each group member uses their notes at home to review the sermon. Remind the group that you will be doing a group review the following week.

PREPARATION

Bible passage from previous week's sermon

LESSON AIMS

To hone the group's skills in listening to and learning from a sermon.

Suggested lesson format

Start with the focus activity.

Read the Bible passage used in the sermon under review.

Discuss what was said, using the suggested format for taking notes from Week 20 and recording the answers on a flip chart or board.

Clarify any misunderstandings.

Discuss the sermon application(s).

Discuss any difficulties experienced by the group and ways of improving their listening and note taking skills.

FOCUS ACTIVITY

Are you ready? Sit the group in a circle and give each person a number. (If you have a large group you might want to form more than one circle.) Ensure that everyone knows their number by asking the group to call out their numbers in turn. One person starts in the centre of the group. He or she spins a metal plate on its edge and calls out the number of one of the other players. That person must run into the centre and catch the plate before it falls to the ground. If the player succeeds in catching the plate he or she returns to their place in the circle. If he fails, he spins the plate and calls out another number.

At the end of the game point out the importance of listening carefully so that the players did not miss their number being called. Also, they needed to respond to what was heard if they were to catch the plate before it stopped spinning. Let's find out what we heard last week and what responses were required.

OVERVIEW
The Sermon on the Mount

Week 23 | **The Christian Character** | *Matthew 5:1-16*
To learn what characteristics should be displayed by a true disciple.

Week 24 | **The Christian and God's Law** | *Matthew 5:17-48*
To learn the importance of keeping God's law in the way he intended.

Week 25 | **The Christian and God** | *Matthew 6:1-18*
To learn the importance of not being hypocritical in our religious practices.

Week 26 | **The Christian and Possessions** | *Matthew 6:19-34*
To learn the proper Christian attitude towards possessions.

Week 27 | **The Christian and Other People** | *Matthew 7:1-12*
To learn the right way to behave towards other people.

Week 28 | **The Christian Response** | *Matthew 7:13-29*
To understand the difference between true and false disciples.

SERIES AIMS

1. To discover more about Jesus' teaching on the Christian life.

2. To learn how this applies to our own lives.

MEMORY WORK

Let your light shine before men, that they may see your good deeds and praise your Father in heaven.

Matthew 5:16

The Sermon on the Mount

The Sermon on the Mount is found in Matthew 5:1 - 7:29. It has the same general outline as the sermon in Luke 6:20-49, but is much more detailed and contains material unique to Matthew. Opinion differs as to whether the sermon is a summary of what Jesus taught on this one occasion, or a compilation of teachings presented on several occasions. Possibly, Matthew took a single sermon and expanded it with other relevant teachings of Jesus.

The theme running through the passage is the Christian life, or discipleship, and these chapters follow on from the call of Jesus' first disciples (Matthew 4:18-22). Jesus outlines to them the privileges and demands of their new calling. It is a sermon addressed to disciples, so it is wrong to ask anyone who is not a Christian to try and practise its teaching. The so called 'social' application of the sermon to modern life is a fallacy, e.g. the section on 'turning the other cheek' is sometimes taken in isolation to mean all forms of war are unchristian.

Matthew wrote his gospel as a Jew who had found in the Lord Jesus the fulfilment of all that was precious in his Jewish heritage. For him it was important to point out the scriptural grounds for seeing Jesus as the Messiah of Israel, whose mission was to fulfil the law and the prophets (5:17).

The lesson divisions are in a way arbitrary, because the underlying theme goes through all six lessons. It is, therefore, important at the start of each lesson to recapitulate on the previous one, in order to reinforce the teaching and see how each lesson fits into the overall theme of the sermon, i.e. the Christian life.

Recommended reading

D.M. Lloyd Jones 'The Sermon on the Mount' IVP
D.A. Carson 'The Sermon on the Mount' Paternoster Press

PREPARATION

Matthew 5:1-16

LESSON AIMS

To learn what characteristics should be displayed by a true disciple.

5:1   See 4:23-25. The crowds were large and looking for healing.

5:2   The teaching was primarily for the disciples (see also Luke 6:20). The whole sermon deals with the life of the disciple, i.e. life in the kingdom of heaven. The 8 Beatitudes are about spiritual things and the associated rewards are also spiritual and can only be completely fulfilled in heaven. In each Beatitude the reward is associated with the characteristic being described.

5:3   The word translated 'blessed' in the NIV is a term of congratulation. Jesus is telling his disciples to strive after these qualities and they will not lose out in the long term.

Poor in spirit is nothing to do with material poverty, but with an acknowledgement of spiritual bankruptcy. (Cf. the tax collector's attitude in Luke 18:13-14.) In the Old Testament this description was used of the people of God who were looking to him for salvation (Isaiah 61:1-2). We need to remind our young teens that we are all unable to save ourselves; we all need to depend on God for our salvation.

The first and last Beatitudes end with the same reward, the kingdom of heaven. This is a literary device called 'inclusion' and signifies that all the material in between is about the same subject, in this case what it means to belong to the kingdom of heaven. The kingdom of heaven contains all those prepared to live under God's rule, therefore these Beatitudes are not just for the 'super-spiritual', but for every Christian.

5:4   This follows on from the previous Beatitude. If we recognise our sinfulness and the evil of the world we live in then we will mourn. This is the opposite of the message being received daily from the world about the importance of the feel good factor.

5:5   There is a difference between the poverty of v.3 and the meekness of this verse. The meek man has a desire to see others advance, do well or benefit, even ahead of himself. The meek man submits himself to God and does not strive for his 'rights'.

5:6   This Beatitude describes the man who seeks to live in a way that conforms to God's will. Therefore, this man delights in God's word because that is where God's will is set out.

5:7   Cf. Ephesians 4:32. Mercy is more than forgiveness; it has to do with the qualities of compassion and gentleness. Christians forgive because they are conscious of being themselves forgiven sinners. Being judgmental is an easy trap for young teens to fall into.

5:8   The heart was considered to be the control centre of the personality, the place where decisions were made. For God's view of the human heart see Matthew 15:19, Jeremiah 17:9. Our hearts can only be made pure by the blood of Jesus. Being pure in heart is not to be confused with outward conformity to a set of rules. We need constantly to ask ourselves to what extent our behaviour mirrors our hearts.

5:9   Cf. James 1:20. Peace makers are those who seek to make peace between God and man and between man and man. The way to make peace between God and man is to tell people the gospel. We should also be seeking to lessen tensions and bring about reconciliation in our daily lives.

5:10   The Christian lives in a sinful world and therefore, if he exhibits genuine righteousness, he will be rejected or mocked by many. Cf. John 15:18-20.

5:11   The persecution that is followed by blessing is persecution because we are Christian, not because of obnoxious behaviour.

5:12   The prophets were persecuted because they told people what God had said.

5:13-15   Salt and light are both metaphors to do with Christian witness in the world. Salt gives flavour and was used as a preservative. Both salt and light can only have an effect if they are distinctive from their environment yet involved in it. Both are no good if they do not fulfil their function.

5:16   If we are not seeking to tell people about Jesus and trying to live lives that demonstrate the truth of what we say, we are not doing our job as Christians.

When teaching this lesson we need constantly to remind ourselves and the group that the characteristics described are not requirements for entry into God's kingdom, but those displayed by people God has already blessed through the gospel.

1. Make a list of the Christian characteristics found in v.3-10. Discuss the precise meaning of each one and identify the barriers that exist to wanting to live this way.

2. Meekness is not weakness (v.5). Should Christians be involved in pressure groups?

3. What do the Beatitudes teach about the importance of attitudes? How should the Christian characteristics described affect the way we treat other people?

Who Am I? Think of 10 different occupations, such as fireman, ballet dancer, nurse, banker, chef, etc. Write a description of each one on a separate piece of card and stick them up around the room. E.g. 'I sometimes work through the night, but never leave the station. My engine is red and quite noisy and I am very brave. I'm not afraid of tall buildings, but have to keep quite fit.' (Fireman)

Give each group member a pen and a piece of paper and ask them to guess the occupations. After a set period of time the one with the most right answers wins. Let's see what the Bible has to say about the characteristics of a Christian.

ACTIVITY

Divide the group into teams and make a set of cards for each team with the Beatitudes divided in the following way:

| Blessed are the poor in spirit | for theirs is the kingdom of heaven. |

Complete the genuine Beatitudes but in addition make a number of 'home made' ones which have Scriptural sounding promises but are not found in Matthew 5. Here are a few examples:

| Blessed are the humble in heart | for they will find rest for their souls. |

| Blessed are the peace keepers | for they will live long in the land that the Lord their God shall give them. |

| Blessed are the faithful | for they will sit at God's right hand. |

| Blessed are the patient | for they will inherit the Elgin marbles. |

| Blessed are those who endure hardship | for perseverance is character building. |

The game is to see how many genuine Beatitudes can be identified with their correct blessings.

PREPARATION
Matthew 5:17-48

LESSON AIMS
To learn the importance of keeping God's law in the way he intended.

5:17 Jesus fulfilled the Law and the Prophets, (the Jewish Scriptures), because they pointed towards him. He was also the only one who could keep the Law completely. He had definitely not come to abolish them and did not see himself in opposition to the OT. E.g. Isaiah 53 speaks in detail of the Messiah's death, a prophecy exactly fulfilled by Jesus' death on the cross.

5:19 Christians are not exempt from keeping the Law. The Christian should seek to live in conformity with God's will in gratitude for what God has done in salvation, not to earn his way to heaven.

5:20 The Pharisees kept the Law meticulously. The only way the Christian's righteousness can exceed that of the Pharisees is by confessing our spiritual bankruptcy and casting ourselves on God's mercy (see Romans 3:21-24).

5:21-47 Jesus gives six examples of the law and the Christian's relationship to it, contrasting it with the false teaching of the teachers and Pharisees of his day.

5:21-26 Wrath, spite and revenge are judged by Jesus as punishable offences on a par with murder. The Jews of the day would have considered themselves not guilty of breaking the 6th Commandment, but here Jesus shows otherwise. They were breaking the spirit of the Law, whilst keeping the letter of the Law.

5:27-30 The Pharisees and teachers had reduced the commandment, which prohibited adultery, to the act itself, ignoring the state of the heart which led to the act.

5:29-30 These verses are not a case for self-mutilation, but a demonstration of the drastic measure needed to deal with sin.

5:31-32 The Jews of the day were interpreting Deuteronomy 24:1-4 very loosely so that divorce could be granted on trivial grounds, e.g. serving a burnt meal to a husband. The Biblical teaching on the sanctity of marriage and God's hatred of divorce is clear (Malachi 2:16).

5:33-37 Again the Jews were guilty of tampering with the Law. The swearing of oaths had degenerated into a complex series of rules which let you know what you could get away with and what you could not avoid. Jesus condemned the flippant use of God's name or a sacred place or object to guarantee the truth of what was spoken.

5:38-42 See Exodus 21:22-25. The law of retaliation was meant to limit the punishment to fit the crime and prevent vendettas. By invoking the law of love Jesus corrected the popular misunderstanding of the law of retaliation. A Christian does not have the 'right' to retaliate and wreak vengeance (v.39), to have possessions (v.40), or to time and money (v.41-42). Personal sacrifice replaces personal retaliation.

5:43-47 Again the teachers of the day had been guilty of tampering with the Law by adding to it. The OT says in Leviticus 19:18, 'Love your neighbour', but nowhere does it say, 'Hate your enemy'. The Jews interpreted 'neighbour' as applying only to other Jews, hence the parable of the good Samaritan in Luke 10:25-37. In the light of Jesus' love for those who persecuted him, (see Luke 23:34), it will not do for us to merely love our friends and leave it at that!

5:48 The conclusion to this passage is 'Be perfect'. Although we can never reach perfection in this life, we should remember that this is God's standard for us.

QUESTIONS

1. In view of these verses why do we need the 'righteousness that comes from God'?

2. Think of the conversations of those around you, e.g. at school. What should be the difference between them and you? How can you control your language?

FOCUS ACTIVITY

Keeping the Rules   Play any well-known game, such as tag, hide & seek, Simon Says, and explain the rules to the group. Prime another 1 or 2 people to play the game, but not to follow the rules. Allow them to cause some disruption.

Discuss the chaos that occurred through breaking the rules. Does the same thing happen when we break God's rules? Let's look at the Bible to find out.

ACTIVITY

Photocopy page 73 for each group member. The verse is from Matthew 5:16.

Memory Verse Puzzle

In this puzzle you must discover which letter of the alphabet is represented by each number. The words only read across, and you have been given one word to start you off.

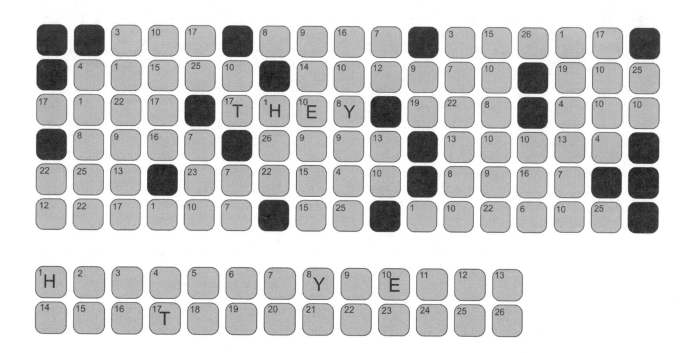

From which verse in the Sermon on the Mount does this come?

PREPARATION

Matthew 6:1-18

LESSON AIMS

To learn the importance of not being hypocritical in our religious practices.

6:1 As with all the titles and headings in the Bible, we must remember that they were put in by the translators. Chapter 5:48 is linked to Chapter 6:1. Chapter 5 ends with the injunction to be perfect but, because we are sinful and self-deceptive, we are warned to seek God's approval rather than man's. There then follows a description of three acts of Jewish piety, including a denunciation of the ostentation of the act, a recognition of the limited results of that false piety and instructions for the right way of doing it.

6:2-4 Giving. The hypocrites (Greek word for actor) do not give to the needy from the heart, but in order to be honoured by men. This is their only reward. These are not real acts of righteousness or genuine piety so there is no reward from God. The real believer should give secretly, both to protect himself from ostentation and pseudo piety and to ensure that he is giving to the Lord.

6:5-15 Praying. This sort of praying is done to get the praise and respect of men, which is its only reward. Jesus mentions two things which should characterise our praying; it should be done in secret and should not consist of meaningless repetition. These verses are not forbidding public prayer (cf. Acts 1:24), nor attacking long prayers. Neither are they commending length and repetition, e.g. 'I prayed so **much** about it, God **must** do .....' When we pray we should be concentrating on God, not on the effect we are having on others present. Then follows the example of prayer, commonly known as 'The Lord's Prayer'.

6:9-13 There is a wealth of comment on this model prayer, but here we are trying to summarise the context and point out the difference between this 'real' prayer and what has gone before. There are 6 petitions, the first 3 concerning God - his name, his kingdom, and his will. The opening title given to God, 'Our Father', points out the new relationship between a father and his children, but to maintain the balance of reverence and awe we are reminded that he is 'in heaven'. The next 3 petitions concern man - his need for food, forgiveness and protection.

6:14-15 If we are not willing to forgive those who sin against us we should question whether we are ourselves forgiven sinners.

6:16-18 Fasting. Jesus here condemns the ostentation of their fasting not the practice. What should have been an occasion for spiritual self-discipline became an occasion of pompous self-righteousness.

QUESTIONS

1. List the religious practices Christians perform, e.g. church/Sunday school attendance, reading the Bible, praying, etc. What should be the motivation for doing them?

2. How should a Christian decide where to give money, time, etc?

3. What help does this passage give for our prayer life? Can you think of any practical things to help you pray correctly, e.g. a prayer diary, writing a letter to God, a list of people to pray for, etc?

Do As I Say! To introduce the idea of hypocrisy, play a game of 'Port & Starboard'. Each side of the room corresponds to the side of a ship; 'port' is the left-hand side of the room looking forward, 'starboard' is opposite to port, 'bow' is the front wall, 'stern' is the back wall. As well, there are various actions for 'climb the rigging', 'scrub the deck', man the lifeboats', salute the captain', etc. The group line up down the centre of the room facing the leader. Every time the leader calls out a command the group members run to the appropriate place or do the action. The last one there is out. The leader stands at the front to demonstrate the appropriate response. Sometimes the leader changes the response, e.g. 'climb the rigging' should be pretending to climb a rope ladder but the leader lies down on the floor ('hit the deck'). Does the group do what you do or what you say? Whether those who obey the command or those who follow the action are out is an arbitary decision. This causes further uncertainty within the group.

Point out that saying one thing whilst doing another is hypocrisy. Jesus warned people of the dangers of being hypocrites. Let's see what he said.

Charades (Give us a clue)

Prior to the lesson choose suitable verses or words from the Bible passage for acting out. Split the group into 2 teams. Allocate each team a number of words or verses. The teams take it in turn to act out the word or verse to the other side. Points are scored by the teams for correct answers.

Use the following actions to indicate what is being acted:

Word - bring hand away from the mouth once.

Verse - bring the hand away from the mouth then, starting with the hands together in front of the mouth, part the hands to demonstrate length, i. e. more than one word.

This activity can be also done using drawings rather than acting.

WEEK 26
The Christian and Possessions

PREPARATION
Matthew 6:19-34

LESSON AIMS
To learn the proper Christian attitude towards possessions.

The central theme of possessions, having already been dealt with in the short sayings in verses 19-24, is continued in the more sustained arguments of verses 25-34. Most of the time we are taken up with the day to day affairs of our lives, often materialistic, but Jesus is challenging us to put God first by giving priority to eternal issues and trusting our Father to meet our needs here on earth.

6:19-21 Points out the foolishness of being permanently concerned with this world's 'treasure', which will not last beyond the grave.

6:22-24 The argument depends on the word play, which the NIV translates as 'good' (v.22), but has a literal meaning of 'single' and denotes generosity. By contrast, 'bad' is a metaphor for stinginess and jealousy. These verses are an attack on selfish absorption with material gain and verse 24 reinforces the call to wholehearted devotion to God. 'Money' comes from the Aramaic word 'Mammon', which is a general term for material possessions, not necessarily ill-gotten gains.

6:25-33 These verses illustrate the point about not worrying by demonstrating God's lavish provision for his creation, i.e. birds and flowers. It is worry that is forbidden here, not responsible provision for the needs of self and family. Even though God provides for the birds, they still have to search for the food! The Christian's proper attitude is to put God first and trust in him for our needs. (NB. It is undoubtedly true that, in today's world, many, including Christians, do not have enough for their needs. This passage does not address that problem, but we need to consider whether it is caused by man's greed and/or man's misuse of God's provision.)

6:34 The final verse of this chapter warns us that provision does not rule out freedom from trouble.

QUESTIONS

1. What is the difference between 'needs' and 'wants'?

2. On whom are you dependent for all your needs? Do you ever consider that person will let you down? What does that teach us about our dependence on God?

3. Is there anything wrong with money? Look up 1 Timothy 6:10 and find out where the problem lies. What can we do to guard ourselves from falling into the kind of temptations that wealth can bring?

Treasure Chest Divide the group into smaller units and give each one a bundle of magazines and newspapers containing a large number of adverts and a large piece of paper in the shape of a treasure chest (see diagram). The groups cut out pictures of things that people, adults or children, would save up their money to buy and glue them onto their treasure chest, such as cars, mobile phones, clothes, holidays. You might want to allocate each group a specific group to collect items for, e.g. boys, girls, men, women.

Discuss the treasures. Let's see what Jesus had to say about our attitude to treasure.

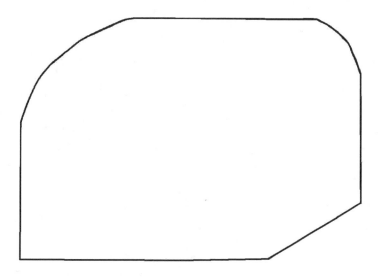

Photocopy page 78 for each group member.

The Bible verse is Matthew 6:21.

Find the following 23 words in the word square. Each word reads in a straight line horizontally, vertically or diagonally and can read backwards or forwards. No letter is used more than once.

BODY   HEAVEN   PAGANS   WEAR
CLOTHES   KINGDOM   RIGHTEOUSNESS   WORRY
DARKNESS   LAMP   RUST   YOU
DRINK   LIFE   SERVE
EARTH   LIGHT   THIEVES
EAT   MONEY   TREASURES
EYE   MOTH

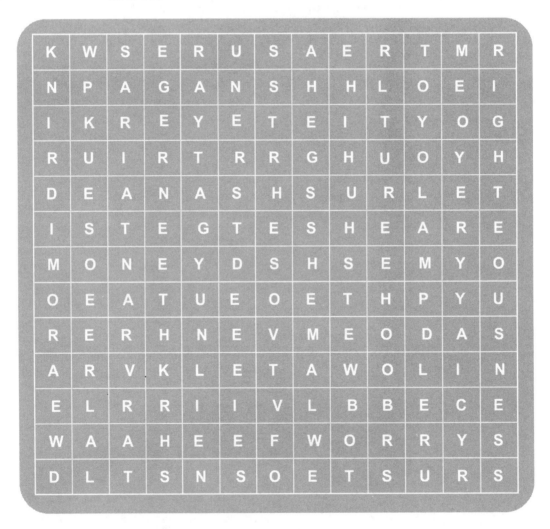

Now, starting from the top and reading from left to right, write down the remaining letters to discover an important fact.

From which verse does this come?

PREPARATION
Matthew 7:1-12

LESSON AIMS

To learn the right way to behave towards other people.

In the previous chapter Jesus has warned us against pseudo-religion, (6:1-18), and materialism, (6:19-34). In this passage he warns us against being judgmental (7:1-5) and encourages us to persist in trusting God with child-like faith (7:7-11). The final verse (12) is a summary.

7:1-5   We are warned about the danger of developing a critical and judgmental spirit. 'Be judged' in verse 1 may well refer to God's judgment as well as that of other people. It is very easy to see faults in other people and much less easy to see those same faults in ourselves.

7:6   There is a right kind of judgment/ discernment which the disciples are instructed to use (see also v.15-20). Sacred or valuable things should only be given to those able to appreciate them. God's truth must not be exposed to unnecessary abuse and mockery (Ecclesiastes 3:7 - there is a time to speak, and a time to be silent).

7:7-11   Persistence in prayer (the verbs are all in the present continuous tense) means we can expect an answer, not because of a technique, length of prayer, time of day, etc. but because it is God who is being approached when we pray. If even human fathers who are evil (all have sinned) can be relied upon to do their best for their children, how much more can God? God only offers us good gifts, the best being his Holy Spirit.

7:12   This rule is found in its negative form in rabbinical literature, Hinduism, Buddhism and Confucianism. It also occurred in various forms in Greek and Roman ethical teaching. Here Jesus is stating it in the positive, which is much more demanding. This verse concludes his teaching on living as a disciple.

QUESTIONS

1. In this passage it seems as though the section on prayer is inserted between passages on dealing with other people. Can you think why that is?

2. What lessons can we learn about prayer from this passage?

3. How would you want other people, (i.e. family and friends), to treat you? Think how that applies to your treatment of them.

FOCUS ACTIVITY

Good Gifts   Divide the group into pairs and ask them to tell each other about the best present they have ever had and who it was from. Share with the larger group. Discuss why we give presents and what this says about our feelings for the recipients. We give good gifts to those we love. Let's see what Jesus said about the way we should treat each other and how God treats us.

ACTIVITY

Photocopy page 80 for each group member.

The word is 'critical'.

Write the words of the Bible verse below into the grid. When you have finished, take the letters from the shaded squares and rearrange them to see what this passage is teaching us not to be.

You hypocrite, first take the plank out of your own eye, and then you will see clearly to remove the speck from your brother's eye.

Matthew 7:5

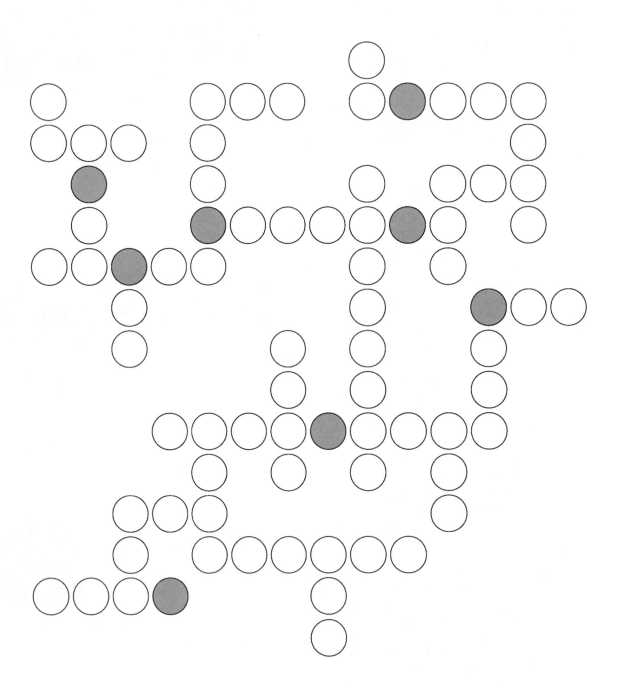

PREPARATION
Matthew 7:13-29

LESSON AIMS
To understand the difference between true and false disciples.

These verses, which contain four contrasts between true and false disciples, conclude the Sermon on the Mount.

7:13-14 There are two gates, one which leads to salvation and life and one which leads to destruction. To choose the narrow gate means going against the mainstream and being in a minority position.

7:15-20 The reason why God allows false prophets is seen in Deuteronomy 13:1-5. False prophets come disguised as true christian leaders but their purpose is the destruction of the flock. Their prophecy is to be tested, not taken at face value. Their fruit is their behaviour (cf. Malachi 2:7-10). Prophecy in the NT primarily means giving a message from God, not predicting the future.

7:21-23 Genuine disciples are those known to the Lord and who 'know' him (have a relationship with him). Acceptance by God does not depend on what we say or do, but on what Jesus has done on the cross. Obviously, we must also bear in mind that 'faith without works is dead' (James 2:26), so real faith is demonstrated in obedient lives.

7:24-27 The difference between the wise and foolish builders is that the wise obey what they hear. They put Jesus' words into practice (cf. the fruit of verses 16-20).

7:28-29 These verses mark the conclusion to the sermon by showing the reaction of the crowd who saw the authority of Jesus, which was in marked contrast to that of other teachers of the day (cf. 5:21-47). This authority was demonstrated not just by the words of the sermon, but also by the miraculous deeds chronicled in the following 2 chapters.

QUESTIONS

1. Summarise the difference between a 'real' believer and a nominal one.

2. How do you develop a relationship with friend? How does that help in understanding your relationship with God?

FOCUS ACTIVITY

True or False? Ask the leaders to think up 2-5 true and false statements about themselves, depending on the number of leaders. The leaders take it in turns to read out their statements. As each one is read out the group has to vote 'true' or 'false' by standing up / sitting down or moving to the appropriate side of the room. The correct answer is announced after each vote. Individual group members keep the score of how many they get right.

In the Sermon on the Mount Jesus talks about 2 groups of people, true disciples and false ones. You are either one or the other, just like in the game. Let's find out how to tell them apart.

ACTIVITY

The quiz can be used to revise the whole series.

Split the group into 2 teams. The teams are told that they are to lay a foundation to build a house. The winner is the first team to get the 6 parts of the rock required for their house's foundation.

Requirements
Each team requires 8 pieces of card (see diagram), 6 coloured grey (rock) and 2 coloured yellow (sand). The pieces of card are randomly numbered from 1 to 8 on the back and are pinned to a board with the numbers showing. The 2 sand coloured cards introduce an element of chance, so that a team member who answers a question incorrectly will not place the team in an irretrievable position.

Rules
A question is put to each team in turn and, if answered correctly, one of the team members chooses a card by calling out its number. The card is turned over and, if grey, is pinned onto the board. Sand coloured pieces are discarded. If an incorrect answer is given the question is offered to the other side.

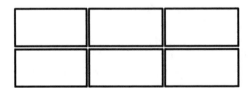

You need a total of 16 questions from the Bible passage, 8 for each team. Allow 10-15 minutes for the quiz.

Bible Timeline

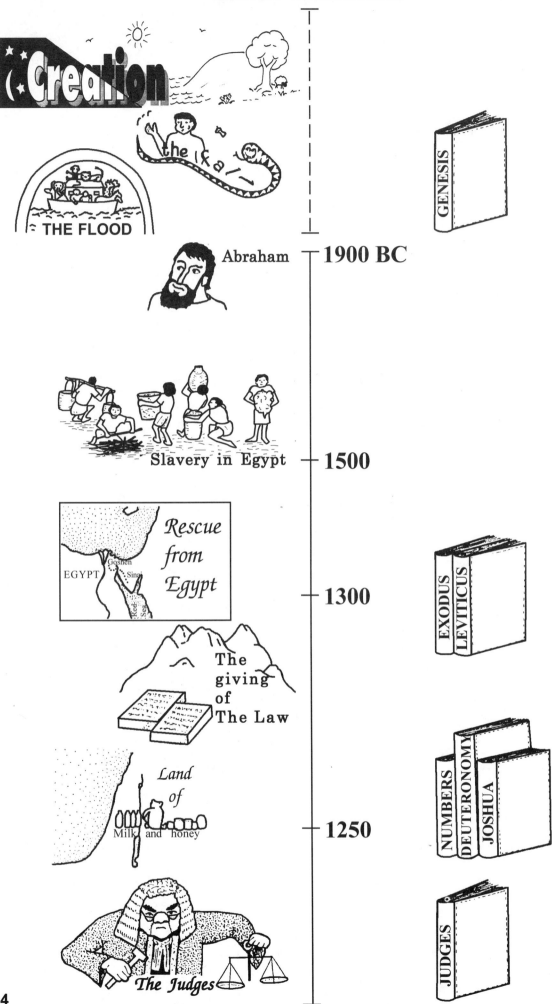

Creation

the fall

THE FLOOD

Abraham — 1900 BC

Slavery in Egypt — 1500

Rescue from Egypt
EGYPT Goshen Sinai Red Sea — 1300

The giving of The Law

Land of Milk and honey — 1250

The Judges

GENESIS

EXODUS LEVITICUS

NUMBERS DEUTERONOMY JOSHUA

JUDGES

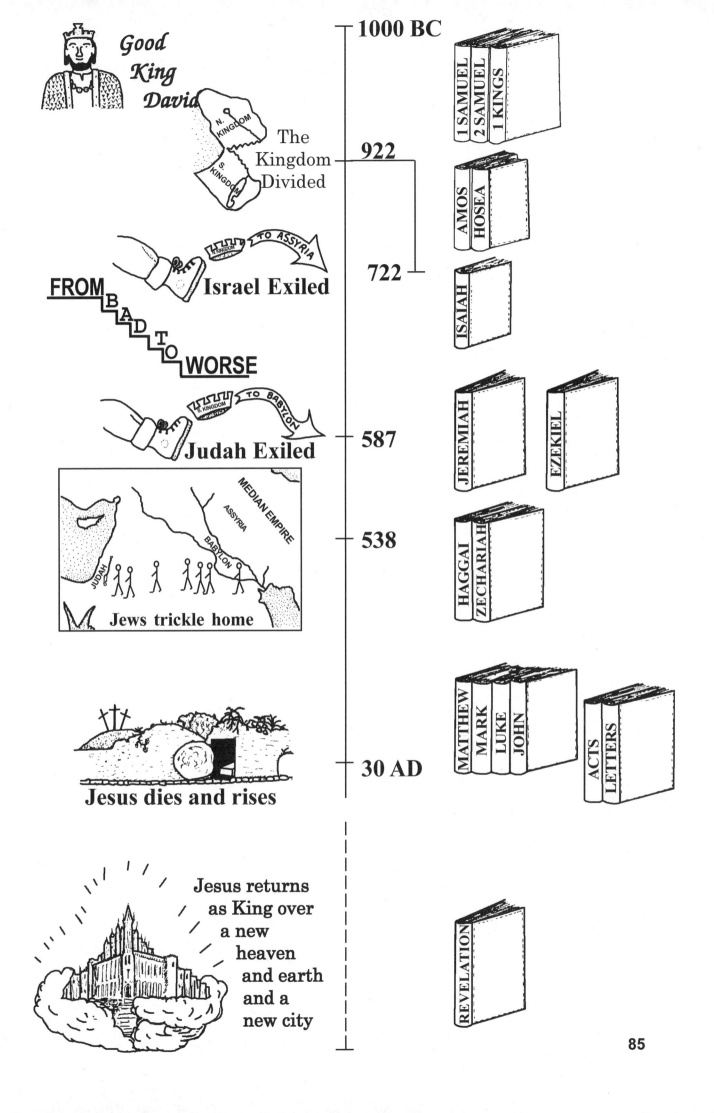

Good King David

The Kingdom Divided

1 SAMUEL 2 SAMUEL 1 KINGS

1000 BC

922

AMOS HOSEA

TO ASSYRIA

Israel Exiled

722

FROM BAD TO WORSE

ISAIAH

S. KINGDOM TO BABYLON

Judah Exiled

587

JEREMIAH EZEKIEL

MEDIAN EMPIRE
ASSYRIA
BABYLON
JUDAH

Jews trickle home

538

HAGGAI ZECHARIAH

Jesus dies and rises

30 AD

MATTHEW MARK LUKE JOHN ACTS LETTERS

Jesus returns as King over a new heaven and earth and a new city

REVELATION

85

Notes   Notes   Notes   Notes   Notes

Notes   Notes   Notes   Notes   Notes

Syllabus for On The Way for 11-14s

Book 1 (28 weeks)	Book 3 (28 weeks)	Book 5 (26 weeks)
Abraham (7) Jacob (7) The Messiah (Christmas) (2) Jesus said, 'I am …' (7) Ruth (5)	Joseph (7) People in Prayer (7) The Saviour of the World (Christmas)(3) Is God Fair? (Predestination) (2) Learning from a Sermon (3) The Sermon on the Mount (6)	Bible Overview (26)
Book 2 (25 weeks)	**Book 4 (25 weeks)**	**Book 6 (27 weeks)**
Rescue (Easter) (3) Paul (Acts 9-16) (7) Philippians (5) Paul (Acts 17-18) (3) 1 Thessalonians (6) Suffering (1)	Psalms (Easter) (2) Paul's Latter Ministry (7) Colossians (5) Choose Life (Hell & Judgment) (2) The Kings (9)	A Selection of Psalms (5) The Normal Christian Life (7) Revelation (9) Homosexuality (1) The Dark Days of the Judges (5)

The books can be used in any order.

The number in brackets indicates the number of lessons in a series.

For more information about *On the Way for 11-14s* please contact:
Christian Focus Publications, Fearn, Tain, Ross-shire, IV20 1TW / Tel: +44 (0) 1862 871 011 or
TnT Ministries, 29 Buxton Gardens, Acton, London, W3 9LE / Tel: +44 (0) 20 8992 0450

Christian Focus Publications publishes biblically-accurate books for adults and children. If you are looking for quality Bible teaching for children then we have a wide and excellent range of Bible story books - from board books to teenage fiction, we have it covered. You can also try our new Bible teaching Syllabus for 3-9 year olds and teaching materials for pre-school children. These children's books are bright, fun and full of biblical truth, an ideal way to help children discover Jesus Christ for themselves. Our aim is to help children find out about God and get them enthusiastic about reading the Bible, now and later in their lives. Find us at our web page: www.christianfocus.com

TnT Ministries

TnT Ministries (which stands for Teaching and Training Ministries) was launched in February 1993 by Christians from a broad variety of denominational backgrounds who were concerned that teaching the Bible to children be taken seriously. The leaders were in charge of the Sunday School of 50 teachers at St Helen's Bishopsgate, an evangelical church in the City of London, for 13 years, during which time a range of Biblical teaching materials was developed. TnT Ministries also runs training days for Sunday School teachers.